FORE PLAY

the very best of playboy's classic golf humor

edited by
Michelle Urry

GPG

GENERAL PUBLISHING GROUP
Los Angeles

Publisher: W. Quay Hays
Editor: Michelle Urry
Managing Editor: Colby Allerton
Art Director: Kurt Wahlner
Production Director: Nadeen Torio
Color and Pre-Press Director: Gaston Moraga

The publisher wishes especially to thank Hugh M. Hefner, Arthur Kretchmer,
Kelli Phox, Tom Staebler, Karen Stevens and Cortez Wells.

Special thanks to Randy Gold, David Lippman and Erik Rothman.

For information:
General Publishing Group, Inc.
2701 Ocean Park Boulevard, Suite 140
Santa Monica, CA 90405

Library of Congress Cataloging-in-Publication Data

Fore Play, the very best of Playboy's classic golf humor / edited by
Michelle Urry
    p.   cm.
    ISBN 1-881649-81-4
    1. Golf - Humor 2. Golf - Humor, Pictorial. I. Urry, Michelle.
    II. Playboy (Chicago, Ill.)
PN6231.G68F87 1995
818'.5402080355 - dc20   95-6779
                                                                    CIP

Printed in the USA
10 9 8 7 6 5 4 3 2 1

General Publishing Group, Inc.

CONTENTS

INTRODUCTION

by Michelle Urry

I adore golf.

The whole idea is hilarious—precision-minded, highly-focused players testing themselves against their own impossible standards of perfection in rich bucolic settings of lush greenery.

For years, PLAYBOY has been poking fun at this pleasurably addictive and frequently taken-much-too-seriously pastime. Golf has grown into the one major sport which—at all levels—can indisputably help make or break careers, marriages, peace of mind, fortunes and friendships. Even the vocabulary is delicious: Twosomes, foursomes, skins games, calcuttas, eagles, birdies. PLAYBOY has commented on all the above with our own special brand of humor.

Featuring award-winning cartoonists Buck Brown, John Dempsey, Alden Erikson, Interlandi, Raymonde, Smilby, Sneyd, Garel, Reilly and Woodman, FORE PLAY provides an irreverent and outrageous diversion. Get ready for a good time. FORE PLAY is sure to brighten your day.

If it doesn't, you need a mulligan.

GOLF
AN INTRODUCTION
BY KEITH ROBINSON

BONK

FORE.

I PLAY GOLF 'CAUSE IT'S LIKE BOWLING OUTDOORS — YOU CAN DRINK AND SMOKE AND, IF YOU RENT A CART, YOU CAN STAY ON YOUR BUTT MOST OF THE GAME!

No one really *likes* to play golf. This is clear from the design of the game: the better you are, the less you have to play. A poor player will hit the ball over a hundred times and be on the course five hours, while a good player will only hit the ball about seventy times and be in the clubhouse draining a cold one in under three hours. Unfortunately, some executives still believe in the myth of the high-powered business golf game, so, for the sake of your career, you better be prepared...

THE CLUBS

- THE 3 WOOD -
Used to tee off on par 4 and par 5 holes, and to throw as far as you can when your ball goes into the lake on the 6th hole.

- THE 5 IRON -
Used to tee off on par 5 holes, and to throw as far as you can when your ball goes into the lake on the 8th hole.

- THE 9 IRON -
To hit the ball onto the green when you're close enough that you could pitch it there yourself underhand (which you can do if everyone else is off behind a tree looking for his ball) and to throw as far as you can when your ball goes into the lake on the 13th hole.

- THE PUTTER -
To hit the ball into the cup when on the green, and to throw as far as you can when you miss a four inch putt.

- THE DRIVER, 2 WOOD, 4 WOOD, 5 WOOD, 1 IRON, 2 IRON, 4 IRON, 6 IRON, 7 IRON, 8 IRON, PITCHING WEDGE, AND SAND WEDGE -
You won't use these. They're there to weight down the bag when you throw it into the lake on the 15th hole.

THE RULES

Real golf is played just like miniature golf, so you don't need to learn any new rules.

TEEING OFF

When teeing off, the ball can fall into one of eleven zones:

1. The That One Doesn't Count Zone
2. The Goddamn Hook Zone
3. The Goddamn Slice Zone
4. The Goddamn It Zone (left)
5. The Goddamn It Zone (right)
6. The Goddamn It to Hell Zone
7. Hmm... Don't Know My Own Strength Zone
8. At Least It Went Straight Zone
9. The I'll Take It Zone
10. The YeeHAW Whoop Whoop Whoop Zone
11. The That's It I Quit If You Want Me I'll Be In the Clubhouse Draining a Cold One Goddamn It Zone

WHEN TO PLAY

When reserving a tee time, remember it can take 5 hours to play...

3 o'clock — COURSE ISN'T TOO CROWDED! — 1st TEE

17th hole — I THINK I SEE MY BALL... — DAMN! THE SPRINKLERS JUST CAME ON!

WARDROBE

Golfers dress like they get their clothes off a dead clown. This is to keep the courses from getting too crowded by scaring off anyone with the least amount of taste.

Some people like the image of snapping their clubs in half over their knees. This will release your anger, bend the clubs a bit, and shatter your kneecap.

PLAYBOY'S PARTY JOKES

*T*WO GOLFERS agreed to play the ball as it lay. On the sixth tee, they were dead even. The first player hit his drive 200 yards down the middle of the fairway. The second shanked his shot over the trees and out onto an asphalt cart path.

"I get free relief from the cart path," the errant player said to his companion as they drove toward their balls.

"Hell, no you don't," his partner barked. "We're playing it as it lays."

Without another word, the second player dropped his friend off at his ball and headed toward the path. The first golfer laughed as he saw sparks fly from the practice swing, then was quickly silenced as a second set of sparks sent the ball flying over the trees, onto the green, landing three feet from the pin.

"Great shot," he shouted. "What club did you use?"

"Your six iron."

"Now do you see why he's never become a champion?"

"Darn! It went in the little hole! That means
I have to wait until number seven before
I get to hit the ball again!"

THE PLAYBOY ART GALLERY

Millet's THE GLEANERS by Jim Beaman

PLAYBOY'S PARTY JOKES

A PROMINENT BUSINESSMAN was sent this ransom message: "If you want to see your wife again, bring $50,000 to the 17th green of the country-club golf course at ten o'clock sharp on Friday morning."

He didn't arrive on the 17th green until noon. A masked man stepped from behind some bushes and growled, "What the hell took you so long? You're two hours late."

"Hey, gimme a break," the husband pleaded. "I have a twenty-seven handicap."

• • •

A GOLF PRO manually guiding a shapely pupil through her swing somehow managed to entangle the back of her skirt in his trouser's zipper. Try as they might, they simply weren't able to separate the two garments, and the fellow and the girl were the object of amused looks from the other golfers as they lock-stepped in some embarrassment toward the clubhouse for assistance.

Just as they reached it, a large dog came racing around a corner of the building and dashed a bucket of water on them.

"Nobody drinks my whiskey, thumps my woman and then brags about bein' a scratch golfer—go get your sticks!"

two years ago, we told you golf would take over the nineties.
now we're telling you it's even more serious than that.
these days, if you don't play golf, you can't talk to the guys, you can't
conduct your business, you can't learn life's important lessons.
because of golf we're not meeting any women. It's driving us crazy. It's . . .

The Golf Crisis

IT'S TRUE. Golf has taken over everything. It has insinuated itself into the otherwise tight twill of our everyday lives. For it, we abjure those things that are responsible, honorable and for which we endured years of arduous training. Golf has become a nonnegotiable demand on our time. And what do we get in return? Golf's current abuse. It used to be immensely rewarding. Here was a relationship we could understand. But lately, golf has been tarted up. Its once wholesome, animal allure is now in danger of losing its soul.

During the seventies, it was trendy for golf architects to build new 7000-yard-long "backbreaker" courses. Existing country clubs joined the bandwagon, stretching out their courses by building new tees farther back into the woods.

Equipment companies assisted golfers desperate for distance by designing the perfect distance combination for long tee shots: metal woods, graphite shafts and solid balls. Business boomed. Golfers, frustrated for years, now lived for the powerful clicking sound a metal head makes when a graphite shaft whips it into the ball at high club-head speed. Then a new architectural trend took place in

ILLUSTRATION BY JOHN O'LEARY

the eighties: shorter, narrower courses that were littered with more sand and deeper bunkers. Equipment companies came to the rescue again, only this time, the focus was on the manufacture of "game-improvement" recovery clubs. An array of high-lofted six, seven and eight woods with unique cambered soles gave the golfer ripping power in the rough.

More technologically advanced investment cast irons, featuring perimeter weighting, were designed to launch the ball high into the air and correct a bad shot hit off the club face's heel or toe.

But lately, golf has been tarted up. Its once wholesome, animal allure is now in danger of losing its soul.

To solve the problem of saving par from treacherous lies around the green, a 60-degree wedge (which looks more like a shovel than a golf club) was marketed. Any shot a golfer couldn't hit with a pitching wedge or a sand wedge the "third wedge" would now play for him.

In 1990, the trend was lightning-fast greens. Putting a ball to a hole on an undulated, slow green is tough enough, but shave a green down so low that the ball rolls like it's on a billiard table and the golfer's nerves become frazzled. Say hello to the long putter. Almost a foot and a half longer, this pole-vault-stick-like club helps a player employ a perfect, pendulum arms-shoulders type of stroke, rather than a hand-wrist action that's more apt to break down under pressure.

The newly designed game-improvement clubs essentially put the golfer's wood and iron game on automatic pilot. High-lofted utility woods slice through heavy grass with the ease of a sickle. The 60-degree wedge is so lofted it can scoop a ball from hell into heaven. The long putter makes a golfer "yip"-proof on the greens. Perfectly mowed fairways allow the player to pick the ball cleanly off grass with the ease of a hockey player hitting a puck off ice, thereby axing the challenge of playing a shot out of a divot, depression or scruffy lie—killing off the art of shot making. The men who introduced golf in America had an entirely different game in mind.

The historical consensus is that golf was first played in America on a cow pasture in Yonkers, New York, in 1888. Soon after, John Reid and his cronies built a six-hole course—called St. Andrews after the hallowed home of golf in Scotland—and later bought 160 acres of land in nearby Hastings-on-Hudson and supervised the building of an 18-hole course and clubhouse.

That original St. Andrews still exists, but because of the expensive face-lift it was given by Jack Nicklaus, the evolution of golf clubs and the other gazillion changes in the industry, Reid would hardly recognize the old course or the game played on it. Which is a shame, because Reid had visions of Americans preserving the Scottish golf tradition.

In its birthplace, everyone loves golf, but it is only a game. It is not a rich man's sport, as it is in this country. The Old Course at St. Andrews, the cradle of golf, is open to the public for $60. In contrast, Pebble Beach, while open to the public, costs $150 for 18 holes.

Part of the raison d'etre of golf for the Scots is the walk. St. Andrews prohibits anything else. For some American golfers, the electric cart is one of nature's perfect forms of locomotion.

Scots play fast. The typical player plans his shot as he walks to the ball, sets up, hits it and walks on. It is an unwritten law at the Old Course to play a round in less than three and a half hours.

To the modern-day American golfer, every shot is a matter of life and death. He dawdles over the ball, examines the lie, paces off the yardage from one of three marker plates to his ball, throws grass up to test which way the one-mile-an-hour wind is blowing, faithfully takes three practice swings to rehearse the perfect swing, waves the club head back and forth a few times, swings, slices and swears. Then he plops down into the cart, tells his buddy it's time to buy a new set of clubs and steps on the gas, zigzagging down the fairway.

The St. Andrews Old Course was not designed by a golf architect. It is natural links land crafted by God. It just happened as golfers played among the rabbit warrens on the lip of the seashore.

The Old Course is naturally rustic and, therefore, the golfer must improvise shots off tricky lies. When the wind blows off the North Sea, the game is even more challenging. But locals, who despise American target golf, are happy to play "wind cheaters," "pitch-and-runs" and the entire range of contrived shots. They play the game as an exercise in serial crisis management.

The most adventurous thing an American golfer could do, to revise his perspective and help diffuse the golf crisis, would be to go out alone and play a round with one club—say a five iron—in the quiet of the early morning or late afternoon. Just to reacquaint himself with the rigor of improvisation. Just to regain the feel of what real golf is all about: imposing your will upon a small ball as you smack it around nature. At its best and at its purest, it's the closest we ever get to playing God.

"the game"

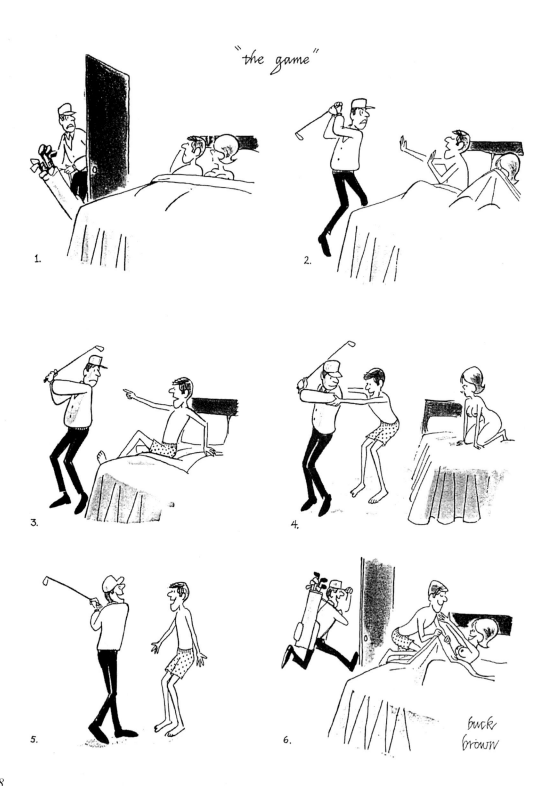

1.

2.

3.

4.

5.

6.

buck
brown

PLAYBOY'S PARTY JOKES

UPON APPLYING for admission to one of the most exclusive country clubs in New England, the rather reserved, unimpressive-looking young man was notified that he must play a round of golf with the club officers as a prerequisite to this acceptance.

On the appointed afternoon, he met them on the first tee equipped with a hockey stick, a croquet mallet and billiard cue. The officers looked him over incredulously, but nevertheless proceeded to tee off. To their dismay, the young man coolly drove 310 yards with the hockey stick, gracefully arched his second shot to the green with the croquet mallet, and sank a 20-foot putt with the billiard cue.

After soundly drubbing the baffled officers with a sub-par 68, the applicant retired with them to the club bar. There he ordered a scotch and soda, and when it arrived, he mixed the drink himself by tossing the contents of the shot glass over his shoulder into the waiting soda behind him on the bar. This further display of the young man's incredible physical condition was too much for the officers of the club.

"You're miraculous," they exclaimed. "What's the story behind these fantastic talents of yours?"

"All my life," the man explained, "physical activity of any sort has been child's play for me. To overcome the boredom that has resulted from my monotonous mastery of everything, I try to do almost everything in the most difficult way possible. Thus, I play tennis with a Ping-Pong paddle, Ping-Pong with a tennis racket, and so on."

"Wait a minute," interrupted one of the club officers. "If it's true, as you say, that you do everything physical in the most difficult manner possible, I have one question. . . ."

"I know," said the talented young man, smiling. "Everyone asks me the same thing and I don't mind telling you. Standing up. . . in a hammock."

"I think we took a wrong turn between the
fifth and sixth holes."

A Conversation
with
Lee Trevino

PLAYBOY: In 1990, you earned one point two million dollars on the Senior Tour, more than Greg Norman made on the regular PGA Tour. The Senior Tour seems to be getting more popular. Why?

TREVINO: The majority of the fans now supporting the Senior Tour watched us play all those years. They've told their kids and the grandkids all about us. That's why our galleries are actually getting younger and younger all the time. Plus, we've always had an identity. Arnold Palmer, the Happy Mex, Chi Chi Rodriguez. We had names and we had people: the little man from South Africa, Gary Player; left-hander Bob Charles; Arnie's Army; the Sergeant, Orville Moody. We were almost like TV characters. The only player on the regular tour galleries identify with and recognize everywhere is Payne Stewart. And that's only because he wears different clothes than everyone else. When he takes those plus fours and those long Argyle socks off, no one knows him. In his private life, he walks around and nobody recognizes him. He's almost like the rock band KISS.

PLAYBOY: It's no secret that the regular PGA Tour needs a

superstar. Candidates include Nick Faldo and Mark Calcavecchia. Can one player dominate?

TREVINO: There are too many tournaments, and the prize money is so big now. No player is going to compete enough to have a chance of dominating. A decent finish in only a couple of events gives him a decent living.

PLAYBOY: Is that the only reason? Isn't it also that today's players lack character?

TREVINO: We're in a different generation. When we came up, in the fifties and sixties, we didn't just play golf. We worked in the pro shop. We sold people shoes. We'd sell a golfer a pair of ten-Ds when he wore eleven-C and he liked them. We sold large-size shirts to guys who wore extra-large. We were salesmen. We went out at night, we drank, we played cards.

> *I looked over at Jack and I said, "Jack, do you mind if I putt out, because if I don't, I'm going to pass out right in the middle of this green."*

The new generation of golfers coming up today is very talented but strictly business. They're not actors—entertainers—and they should be. Regardless of what you think, people still love to be stroked a little bit. They don't care if it's a lie, they just say, "Hey, the guy talked to me." "He slapped me on the back." "We laughed together." "We had a beer." Because of our backgrounds, and because the Senior Tour is like a second childhood, we enjoy ourselves. We love to win, but we have fun doing it. We're entertainers—and people love us more for it.

PLAYBOY: Your first wife called you a golf bum. Is that still an apt description?

TREVINO: I'm still a golf bum, except the income is a little better. I love to play the game. Nothing pleases me more. When I take off to relax, I play golf or hit golf balls. When I sleep at night, I dream about golf. When I'm awake during the middle of the night, I think about the golf swing. It's on my mind all the time. I'm just in love with the damn game.

PLAYBOY: In the early days, you used to bet with no money in your pocket. You must have been scared. Once you started making big bucks on tour, were you ever truly scared during a tournament?

TREVINO: Well, yes. Most players fixing to win a golf tournament, or leading a golf tournament, are scared.

PLAYBOY: Is there one incident you can think of when you were very scared?

TREVINO: In 1974, when I won the PGA at Tanglewood, in North Carolina. I remember playing with Hubert Green and Jack Nicklaus in the last round, and I had what you call the "putting yips." I couldn't take the putter back, and I was having a tough time making any putts in that round. But I hit the ball so well from tee to green and was so close to the hole all the time that a blind man could have made the putts. On the seventy-second hole, I knew that if I two-putted from twenty-five feet, the tournament was mine. But, coming off a three-putt on the seventy-first hole, I was nervous.

I putted the ball down about a foot and a half from the hole. It is customary to mark your ball and let the other players finish, so you can take all the glory when you make yours. But I looked over at Jack and I said, "Jack, do you mind if I putt out, because if I don't, I'm going to pass out right in the middle of this green." Jack looked at me with that little grin of his and said, "Go ahead," and I tapped the ball in. Hell, I had such a case of the yips that if my ball had been two feet away, there was no way I'd have made the putt.

PLAYBOY: Is the pressure-choke factor overrated among golf pros? Have you ever choked?

TREVINO: I don't think it's overrated. You choke when your confidence level is less than one hundred percent, usually due to hitting the ball poorly. You know you're "leaking oil" and it's a matter of time before you break down. There are so many elements to good play, and so much pressure on tour, choking is common.

At Houston one year, I was leading David Graham by one stroke after three rounds, but I was playing poorly. It was so bad on the final day that when I walked to the first tee, I had enough cotton in my mouth to knit a sweater. I took this cup of water, and by the time I got it to my lips, there was no water in it. That's how bad I was shaking. I was so nervous that I was duck hooking. I knew I wasn't striking the ball well enough to win. So I choked. Graham, on the other hand, was playing so well he was choke-proof; he shot sixty-four and won.

PLAYBOY: Many pros say you are the best shot maker of all time. Is there a shot that you can't hit?

TREVINO: Yeah, there are a lot of shots I can't hit. One that comes to mind real quick is a high-draw one iron. In his heyday, Sam Snead was very good at hitting that shot. Today, Nicklaus is very good. The reason: He's tall and a naturally more upright swinger. The size of a golfer has a lot to do with his versatility as a shot maker. I'm short, five foot seven. I can hit a low shot probably easier than a tall player. That's because my swing is more rounded, flatter, and I hold the angle of my hands longer in the hitting area. Therefore, I hit the ball more on the through-swing than on the upswing.

The other shot that gives me trouble is the fairway-bunker shot. Nicklaus is one of the best at executing that shot—if not *the* best. Jack is so good out of a fairway bunker because he *always* hovers the club above the ground, so he feels comfortable in sand, where *Rules of Golf* forbids you to ground the club. Also, he is a natural picker of the ball. I'm more of a digger. I take divots. And diggers make poor fairway-bunker players.

PLAYBOY: Is not being able to hit the high shot what hurts you most at Augusta—where the greens are fast-running—and is being able to hit the low shot what helps you during the British Open when the wind howls?

TREVINO: Exactly. That's why I have no green jackets hanging in my closet but have won the British Open twice. Augusta is like teeing out of a hole all the time. Every tee ball in Augusta is almost going uphill. Then it gets out there, about two hundred fifty, two hundred sixty yards, and then it goes back downhill. I'm not long enough to get over the up, so I'm usually left with a long iron off a hilly lie. The big hitter is strong enough to get over the up. He gets roll and leaves himself a short iron to the green; that's a big advantage, because those clubs are easier to hit with backspin. Augusta is just not a very good golf course for me. Besides, most of the greens at August lean from left to right, which means it takes a right-to-left draw shot to stop the ball quickly. If you go into an Augusta green working the ball from left to right, as I do, the damn thing rolls off the green.

PLAYBOY: Handicap your game.

TREVINO: Driving, probably the top three in the world. So I'm definitely scratch with the driver.

PLAYBOY: Putting?

TREVINO: Uh, two.

PLAYBOY: Sand play?

TREVINO: About a one.

PLAYBOY: Chipping?

TREVINO: Probably scratch.

PLAYBOY: Long irons?

TREVINO: Probably a six.

PLAYBOY: Short irons?

TREVINO: Scratch.

PLAYBOY: Medium irons?

TREVINO: One.

"Damn it, Miriam—you know weekends are for golf!"

PLAYBOY: What would you be doing now if you hadn't become a golf pro?

TREVINO: I'd probably be making license plates—pretty license plates, too. Golf and the Marine Corps have been my salvation.

PLAYBOY: What will you do when you're too old to compete?

TREVINO: If I don't die before I retire, I'm going to teach my craft of shot making to others. Somebody's got to teach younger people how to execute these shots, and I'd like that somebody to be me. I don't want to die with the knowledge I have of hitting different golf shots.

PLAYBOY: That's the sad thing about Ben Hogan. He was a shot-making wizard, but, unlike the great Bobby Jones, who made a series of instruction films, Hogan has left golfers very little.

TREVINO: Exactly! If Hogan were to do a clinic on the day of a senior tournament, I'd withdraw from it.

It's tragic. He's going to leave us someday without at least recording his swing secrets. He was a human shot-making machine and golfers should be treated to more than the one excellent book he wrote, *Ben Hogan's Five Lessons in Golf.*

He *does* make a beautiful golf club, but that doesn't mean anything. He needs to relate his knowledge of shot making to golfers so they can enjoy using his clubs. But maybe he *did* do something like Jones, and he has it locked up in a safe, and when he passes away, they'll bring 'em out. I certainly hope so.

PLAYBOY: You've been accused of using gamesmanship on opponents. Tell us about playing against former British Open and U.S. Open winner Tony Jacklin in England.

TREVINO: The English thought I was crazy because I talked and played golf at the same time. Everything is hush-hush over there. I remember Jacklin saying, "Now, listen, Lee, let's play golf today, I don't want to talk." And I said, "Tony, you don't have to talk, all you have to do is listen."

PLAYBOY: Didn't you throw a fake snake at Nicklaus before the start of the play-off for the 1971 U.S. Open—which you ended up winning?

TREVINO: Oh, that was just a joke. Golf's supposed to be fun. People have said that I do these things to disturb people, but I never tried to do anything like that. Besides, if you're not capable of beating that other guy, whatever the hell you say to him—with the exception of screaming on his backswing—you're not going to beat him.

PLAYBOY: People must have tried to play tricks on you. What are a couple of those tricks?

TREVINO: Talking during my backswing and purposely casting

a shadow on my putting line are two favorites. Or a player who is away and putting on your line pulls the ball left of the hole and tries to put you off by saying, "God, I couldn't believe that goes left!" Or a player mis-hits, say a seven iron, the ball falls short of the green and he says to his caddy, "Boy, I killed that." What usually happens is, an opponent with rabbit ears hears this, chooses a stronger club and hits the ball way over the green. There are a hundred tricks.

PLAYBOY: What was your greatest golf hustle?

TREVINO: God, you know, I never hustled anybody. I was a good player. If I ever hustled anyone, it was merely because I told everybody that I was a scratch player when, truthfully, I beat par by four strokes on my course, Tenison Park, almost every time. So, to tell you the truth, I should have given my opponents more shots on my course. . . because of "local knowledge."

PLAYBOY: Have you ever played with anybody who was truly a born cheat?

TREVINO: Jesus, I played with guys at Tenison Park who did things like put petroleum jelly on the face of the club to make the ball go straight. Oh, hell, these guys were such cheats that we had a rule: You could tee it up everywhere—the rough, bunkers—so you never had to watch the other guy. Let everybody cheat. That way, nobody could outcheat anybody else.

PLAYBOY: Pros shoot in the sixties all the time. Why can't most amateurs break ninety?

TREVINO: Well, rank beginners have no business playing a golf course. I mean, would a guy who just learned to drive enter the Indianapolis 500? People buy a set of clubs, shoes, pay a greens fee and then go play on a golf course. They're wasting time. You've got to get on the practice tee and take lessons. If you're a total beginner, you should practice a year before you ever get on a golf course. You should go to a driving range religiously, three or four times a week, at night, whatever. All weekends should be spent hitting golf balls. Learn how to get the ball in the air; learn how to chip it; get out of bunkers; then you'll enjoy the game. How in the hell are you going to enjoy the game rolling it around? It's not bowling, you know.

PLAYBOY: In France, players must pass written and performance

> *PLAYBOY: Who would be in your ideal foursome?*
>
> *TREVINO: Jesus Christ, Arnold Palmer and Bob Hope.*

tests, and if they fail, they can't play on a regulation course. Should we do the same thing here?

TREVINO: No. I can understand France. France's golf has gone berserk. I can remember ten years ago, they had forty thousand golfers registered with the French Federation of Golf. Now they have two hundred thousand. They haven't been able to increase the number of golf courses that much. But I think golfers here should work at their game more. That's why golf is so slow today, because we have so many players who are shooting such high scores.

PLAYBOY: You've played with Prince Rainier, President Ford, Bob Hope, Sean Connery, the king of Morocco—the list goes on. Who would be in your ideal foursome?

TREVINO: Jesus Christ, Arnold Palmer and Bob Hope.

PLAYBOY: In 1969, at the Hartford Open, you met an eleven-year-old lemonade-stand girl, never dreaming you would marry her in 1983. Assuming that was your greatest golf moment, was your second your Skins Game hole in one—the stroke that earned you one hundred seventy-five thousand dollars and a car?

TREVINO: No, it was when I beat Nicklaus in a play-off to win the 1971 U.S. Open. I shot sixty-eight. He shot seventy-one.

PLAYBOY: Your favorite golf course, Cypress Point, withdrew from the PGA Tour tournament roster because it didn't want to be told whom to let into its club—such as black members. How do you react to that?

TREVINO: I've always had mixed emotions about it. They have two hundred and fifty members. That's why it's so private. Players were never allowed in their clubhouse when we played the Crosby. We usually changed our shoes in the parking lot. But we understood that. We were just appreciative and thankful that we could play a golf course like that. They could have closed the doors on us a long time ago. They kept them open because of Crosby. I'll tell you how exclusive this club is. The parking lot holds about twenty cars. It's a beautiful place. It's always been my favorite, but I never got into this other business. It's a private club, and that's why they call it a private club. So I don't have anything against their saying it's a private club.

PLAYBOY: Describe your prejudices on golf architecture.

TREVINO: Unlike Nicklaus, who builds difficult courses, I believe in building golf courses like the old architects built. I like flat greens and shallow bunkers; I like to leave at least two-thirds of the green open in front where you can bump and run—naturally, because I hit low. I like to put water on a golf course, but I want it to be seen; I don't want it to be in your way. If you hit a real poor shot, there should be a chance of going into the water. But I don't think that you should hit a marginal shot that looks like it's going to go onto the green, and all of a sudden—boop!—it goes into the water. Basically, I build player-friendly courses.

Architects today forget that the majority of golfers are eighteen to twenty-four handicaps. That's one of the reasons that most of the new clubs around the country are going broke—they're too difficult to play. Why should a member and his wife buy a house on a golf course they can't play?

PLAYBOY: The National Golf Foundation projects that about four hundred golf courses a year will have to be built before the year 2000 to accommodate the forty million golfers who will be playing the game. Environmentalists are blocking a lot of new projects.

TREVINO: Sure. They'll kill you in a minute. I wanted to invest in one in Florida, but they had a little mouse or something running around the beach, and it killed us. But we've got some courses going in Taiwan, one in Japan, fixin' to open one up in Wisconsin, so we're getting into a little more all the time.

PLAYBOY: What's the state of golf jokes these days?

TREVINO: I heard one about a guy that had a different-color golf ball that he couldn't lose. I say, "How come you can't lose it?" He says, "Because if you hit it down the fairway, it beeps. You hit it in the rough and a little sickle comes out of it and mows the grass down, where you can see it. If you put it in the water, pontoons come out of it, the wind blows it over and you can retrieve it." I say, "Where in the hell did you buy this thing?" He says, "I don't know. I found this one."

PLAYBOY: Because most golfers don't break ninety, it seems new clubs will not help Mr. Average a great deal. If you agree, don't you feel sort of guilty sponsoring or endorsing Spalding clubs?

TREVINO: I don't think that I should feel guilty about taking money for endorsing a golf club. What Spalding is trying to do is to sell a product that it thinks is better than anyone else's. Everyone else is doing the same thing. That's business. Besides, golfers want to play with what the pros play with.

PLAYBOY: What's in your golf bag?

TREVINO: Listen, my caddy Herman Mitchell knows if my golf bag has an extra golf ball in there; he can tell by the weight of it. There ain't much in there. I carry my rain suit, three gloves and six balls.

PLAYBOY: Are you superstitious about anything?

TREVINO: I don't use a yellow tee. Yellow is the color of weakness, cowardice. I'd hit a ball off the ground with a three wood before I'd use a yellow tee.

PLAYBOY: When it comes to golf clubs, are you fickle?

"Keep your eye on the ball, dear."

TREVINO: Yes. I'm always looking. My caddy gets mad at me because even when I have a driver that I hit extremely well, I take a strange driver out there to try it. I'm always looking for that one jewel.

PLAYBOY: What's the most important part of a golf club?

TREVINO: The shaft, no question. It's the hardest to replace. So if you break the head of a wooden club, keep the shaft.

PLAYBOY: Have you made any changes in your game since joining the Senior Tour?

TREVINO: Yes, I cut most of the forward press out of my putting stroke. I set my hands ahead of the ball and swing the putter back simultaneously, with my hands and the handle. I get a much better roll of the ball.

PLAYBOY: Are you having the most fun you've ever had in your life?

TREVINO: This is heaven. There's nothing better than this. If I had to do it all over, I wish I had been born fifty years old and come right onto the Senior Tour.

PLAYBOY: Defend the proposition that while Nicklaus is probably the greatest golfer of all time, you are the most popular.

TREVINO: Well, I think that I'm *one* of the most popular. Fuzzy Zoeller is very popular. Chi Chi Rodriguez is very popular. No player who's ever played the game has been more popular than the king, Arnold Palmer. I have seen more people watch Palmer pack the trunk of his car in a tournament than watch another player, who is leading, putt out on eighteen. That's the truth! The man has charisma! He's got the people; they love him; I love him; I don't know any professional golfer who doesn't love him.

PLAYBOY: Are you uneasy about the number of Japanese take-overs of American courses?

TREVINO: As long as there's a stipulation that says a golf course must stay a golf course, I don't have a problem with it. Don't be afraid in selling to the Japanese. They can't cut it out of the ground and take it home to Tokyo; they gotta leave it here.

PLAYBOY: What will golf be like in 2001?

TREVINO: Bigger and better. Golf is a sport that everyone is going to be playing. We'll have probably fifty or sixty million players. We'll have to go way out into the sticks to play. I predict we're going to build golf courses in areas where nothing grows, where the property has no value whatsoever. That's where you are going to have to play.

— JOHN ANDRISANI

"Was that three or four strokes, Mr. Bishop?"

PLAYBOY'S PARTY JOKES

IT HAD BEEN a case of definite but controlled attraction to each other at the singles resort, and the 30ish Sun Belt couple were rationally discussing their possible marriage. "In all fairness, Kay," said he, "I should tell you that I'm a golfaholic. I play late afternoons in the spring, summer and fall, and every Saturday and Sunday year-round."

"Thank you for your frankness, Nelson," said she. "In the same spirit of candor, I should tell you that I'm a hooker."

"I wouldn't worry about that," smiled the man. "Just remember to keep your backswing smooth and your wrists straight."

• • •

WHILE ON VACATION in Africa, the traveler entered his hotel's handicap golf tournament. He told the starter that his handicap was 15, and he was assigned a caddy who carried not only his clubs but a rifle as well.

On the first hole, the golfer hit into the tall grass. As he was looking for his ball, he was pounced on by a lion, but his caddy quickly aimed his rifle and killed the animal.

On the second hole, the shaken duffer hit into a thick stand of trees. Searching for the ball, he was attacked by a leopard. Again, the caddy killed the beast.

On the par-three third hole, the golfer hit into the lake in front of the green. He reached down to retrieve the ball, but he was grabbed by a crocodile. This time, the caddy stood by without raising his gun. The frantic fellow beat the croc on the head with his golf club until it finally let go.

Climbing up the bank, the golfer turned to the caddy. "Damn, why didn't you shoot?"

"Bwana, with a 15 handicap, on a par three you get no extra shots."

"You want to bet that when I get home Alice will want me to take her shopping in this lousy weather?"

PLAYBOY'S PARTY JOKES

*H*ARRY, A GOLF ENTHUSIAST if ever there was one, arrived home from the club to an irate, ranting wife.

"I'm leaving you, Harry," his wife announced bitterly. "You promised me faithfully that you'd be back before noon and here it is almost nine P.M. It just can't take that long to play 18 holes of golf."

"Now wait," said Harry. "Let me explain. I know what I promised you, but I have a very good reason for being late. I got up at the crack of dawn, as you know, and picked up Fred at six A.M. But on the way to the course we had a flat tire, and when I changed it, I discovered that the spare was flat, too. So I had to walk three miles to a gas station to get the tire fixed and then roll it all the way back and put it on the car. After that, we got back into the car, drove a quarter of a mile and ran out of gas. I had to trudge all the way back to the gas station and back to the car again. Finally we got to the course and started to play. Everything was fine for the first two holes and then, on the third tee Fred had a stroke. I ran back to the clubhouse but couldn't find a doctor. And, by the time I got back to Fred, he was dead. So for the next 16 holes, it was hit the ball and drag Fred, hit the ball and drag Fred. . . ."

"Go ahead and putt… it'll be a few minutes before
the shock wave hits us."

MASTER OF THE BALL HAWKS

fiction **By PATRICK McGIVERN**

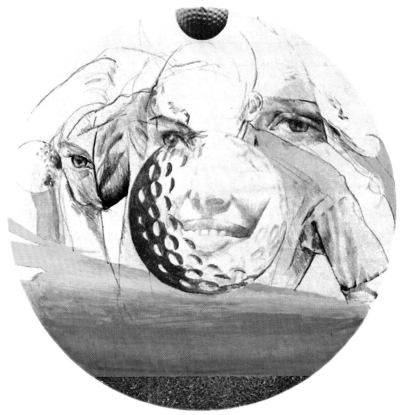

*perfection was what he was looking for—in those hard little
white spheres and in the soft curves of a woman*

ONE DAY, Bertie McKeon would be up there competing with the
best in the Masters Tournament. But we find him now in his forma-
tive years, on a summer afternoon, standing—and waiting—on a hill
that overlooks the grass sward that is the 14th link of the public golf
course in Van Cortlandt Park, the Bronx, New York City.

Bertie does not even know yet that he will become a master
golfer, only that something draws him repeatedly back to the links,
something that excites him, that makes his insides buzz.

Right now, at the age of 12, he believes he is here, like the other
ball hawks, to retrieve and pocket the golf balls that stray off the
links to his side of the fence. Selling the strayed balls is a very

lucrative activity, one that Bertie hopes will help him get some golf clubs—his first—this summer.

But Bertie has not been too successful at finding the lost white treasures. That is why he is waiting for the master of the ball hawks.

Unlike the other ball hawks, the master does not carry a long stick to poke the grass with. And where the others move at a snail's pace, methodically probing, the master strides at what amounts to a trot—the better, Bertie knows, to keep up with the Irish setter that invariably accompanies his patrols, running ahead of him like a galloping flame.

The master is younger than the others, too—30 or 35, to their 50 or 60. And yet, with all these differences, he always manages to find three stray balls to every one they find; and to top everything, he throws most of them away!

It is magic the master works, and Bertie wants to learn the magic. That is why

It is magic the master works, and Bertie wants to learn the magic. That is why he holds the three Dunlop Gold Cups in his hands. He will pay to learn.

he holds the three Dunlop Gold Cups in his hands. He will pay to learn.

And now, here comes the master, right on time, as Bertie knew he would be, the great dog gamboling ahead of him. Bertie steps down the hill on an intercept path, and his heart is heavily thumping. Will he have the nerve to speak?

"Hey, mister. What kind of dog is that?"

"Irish setter."

"I have a dog like that."

"An Irish setter?"

"No, but he's like that. Except he isn't red."

"No kidding?"

Bertie never noticed before, but the master has a very mournful face. He falls into step beside him.

"And he has short hair," Bertie says, "not that kind."

"Yeah?"

"And he's just about half that one's size."

"But otherwise, just like him?"

"Yeah."

The master has stopped in his tracks. He looks hard to his left. He starts off again, this time on a slightly altered course uphill. A few paces and he stops, bends, picks up a golf ball.

"Wilson K-twenty-eight," he says, examining it with a frown. "It'll do, I guess." He sticks the ball into his pocket and resumes his walk.

"Mister?"

"Yeah."

"Will you teach me how to find golf balls?"

"Teach you how to what?"

The master's mournful expression has changed to one of disbelief.

"I'll pay," says Bertie, exhibiting the three Dunlop Gold Cups.

"I don't know anything about finding golf balls, kid."

"You're the best ball hawk there is."

"Ball hawk. What the hell is a ball hawk?"

"You are. You're the master. Better than any three others."

"You mean those guys with the sticks?"

"That's right. You make them look silly."

"Listen, kid, this isn't really my line. I'm not a ball hawk. I'm a commercial artist, albeit a temporarily unemployed commercial artist."

"You find the balls and you take them home, don't you?"

"Yeah, but—"

"Then you're a ball hawk."

"All right, then. I'm a ball hawk."

Bertie knows it is going to be tough dealing with the master. After all, why should he reveal his secrets to anyone? But Bertie is determined to press on.

"Teach me how to find golf balls," he pleads. "I can't find many myself. I wear glasses. I'm slow. Somebody else sees them first or gets them first. I never get any, except sometimes. I got these ones. You can have them if you teach me!"

"Kid—"

"I'll give you two U.S. Royals, also. Please, mister, please!"

The master stops in his tracks again and turns to the boy. He looks not mournful now but intent. "You really want to know how to find golf balls?" he asks.

> *Every man in his mind's eye sees the shape of the perfect woman—her face, her body, even her soul. Every man looks for her, some knowingly, some not knowing, but every man looks.*

"I have six Spalding Dots at home that I will also throw in."

"Sit down."

Bertie sits.

"Close your eyes."

Bertie does.

"Imagine in your mind a golf ball. Round. White. Perfect."

Bertie tries; finally the image comes.

"See it whole, entire. Count each one of its concave facets. Got it?"

"Wait. . . yeah, yeah, I've got it."

"Now let the ball recede, back off from you, off, way off, until it is only a tiny dot in the distance. Now bring the ball back. Slowly, slowly. Now let it recede again. And remember, remember how round it is, how glistening white, how perfect. See it now on a green field, a round whiteness on a green field, now big and up close, now far away and small, but always round, always perfect. Roll the ball up and down the field, smoothly, smoothly. Think of it white, think of it round, now this size, now that. Keep doing it, OK? Now. . . open your eyes and look around."

Bertie does.

"Look over the bridle path and up the hill. First to the right, then to the left."

"It's very confusing," says Bertie.

"Sure, you can see rocks, the bottoms of beer cans, white bits of paper, a thousand things that could be golf balls."

"I think I see one!"

"Look at it again. Remember the perfect white ball you imagined. Perfect roundness, that's what you're looking for. And whiteness, unblemished. Don't settle for anything else. Look again."

Bertie looks again. In contrast to the unsullied green link beyond the fence, the field rising up before him is littered with picknickers' rubble—bottles, beer cans, bits of paper, as the master said. And much of it quite like, but not exactly like, the perfect white roundness in his mind.

"It isn't a ball," he says.

"Most of them are not," says the master. "Using my method, you eliminate a lot of needless effort. You don't run off on a hundred wild-goose chases. You see, it's an old principle you're observing, kid. They call it keeping your eye on the ball. You probably don't know, but it's sort of like with a woman."

Bertie notices that the master looks mournful again.

"Every man in his mind's eye sees the shape of the perfect woman—her face, her body, even her soul. Every man looks for her, some knowingly, some not knowing, but every man looks. And when he finds her, recognition is instant. And he marries."

Bertie's eyes run once more over the field in his view. With the perfect ball in his mind's eye, he can now dismiss, one after another, all the ball-like objects that—before the master's lesson—would have made his heart leap in false discovery. But he sees something else now—a little spot of white near a dirt ridge that runs along the bridle path. No matter how long he looks, the white stays uniform and whole, and the roundness, even at 45 yards, is perfect.

"I see a ball!" he says, and points it out to the master.

"Yes," says the master, "it seems to me that that is quite definitely a golf ball. Go get it."

Bertie does; and when he comes back, he turns it over to the master.

"Hmmmmm," says the master. "A Dunlop sixty-five. . . too bad." And with a disdainful flip, he throws it away. And the white pellet bumps silently down the slope, to land at the heels of another ball hawk.

"What did you do that for?"

"It was nicked," says the master. "Didn't you see that?"

"So what?"

"So they're no damn good if they're nicked."

Even if he is the master, Bertie is appalled. So this is why he throws the balls away!

"Why are they no good if they're nicked?" he demands.

"It's like the perfect woman, kid. Every facet's got to be perfect, perfectly white, perfectly round, spanking new. Otherwise, how the hell can you marry her? Right?"

"You could play with that ball," says Bertie.

"I don't play golf."

"You could sell it, even with the nick."

"I don't need the money."

"Well, what do you do with the balls you keep?"

"I just take 'em home, I guess, put 'em in an old beach bag."

To Bertie's relief, that other ball hawk has finished his probing below them, moving on down the bridle path, the white pellet of the discarded Dunlop gleaming in the black cinders behind him.

"What do you put 'em in a bag for?" asks Bertie.

"I don't know, kid," the master says mournfully. "A compulsion, maybe. Like with women. I like perfect things. I always have. I can't stand flaws. Golf balls. Etchings. Women. Women. Women."

"They have to be perfect, too?"

"They've got to be."

"Of course it's a game we can both play—
Here, carry these and be quiet."

"Why?"

"Kid, you start out in life with certain ideals, certain pictures in your mind's eye, you can't just throw them away because of a—"

"That's a good ball down there. Even with the nick, I could get fifty cents for it. A good golfer could take that ball and whack it two hundred yards, I bet. And a good putter could sink it from forty feet. You could win the Masters Tournament with that ball."

"But it's got a nick in it."

"If all you do is take 'em home and put 'em in a bag, what do you care if it's got a nick in it or not?"

> "That's a good ball down there. Even with the nick, I could get fifty cents for it. . . . You could win the Masters Tournament with that ball."

Another ball hawk is now moving up along the bridle path and Bertie knows he will reach the discarded Dunlop in a matter of minutes. But the master is speaking, or rather mumbling, and he looks more mournful than ever now.

"You won't understand this, kid, but somebody has to hear it. You see, there's this woman I know, a really great woman, in all senses of the word. Except she just don't fit what I want to wind up with. She's a brunette, for God's sake, and another twenty years or so, she may even have a mustache. As if that's not bad enough, this woman, Gladys, she's not even educated! She's a nurse, a dumb nurse; she thinks Oliver Twist is a pastry recipe, that the theory of relativity is about family togetherness. And. . . her ankles are just a bit too thick. What would you do with a woman like that?"

"I don't know what you do with women."

"I do love her, you see. I'm crazy about her. That's what I don't understand. She's pretty, but she's not a blonde. Levelheaded, but dumb. Feminine enough, but not altogether compliant. In short, she's full of nicks. What do you do with a woman like that? It's driving me nuts, I tell you, I don't eat, I don't sleep. I don't care about anything but her. When I walk, I'm six inches off the ground. When I see my friends, all I can talk about is her. Wherever I am, I see her, hundreds of her; only, at the last moment, it's always someone else. I lost my job over mooning about her. And I never want to see her again!"

"Why not?"

"Are you nuts? She's full of nicks. Brunette, thick ankles, dumb. I can get any damn woman I want, and the ones I want have got to be round, white, perfect!"

"If you've got those kind, why don't you marry one?"

"Because they're so great I want to marry them all."

"But you never do."

"No."

"Why don't you learn to play golf?"

"What has that got to do with anything?"

"I don't know," mutters Bertie, but his mind is now on other things: namely, the advancing ball hawk down the slope from them. "Look, mister," he says, "thanks for the lesson. It sure seems to work, that trick." And Bertie hands the master three Dunlop Gold Cups and two U.S. Royals. "Your pay," he says. "And I've got to run. Otherwise, that guy will beat me to the ball I found."

"Hey," the master calls after him. "I'll keep one of these U.S. Royals, but all the others got nicks in 'em."

"Thanks again," says Bertie, snatching up the ball on the cinder path. "They're all yours."

In the course of this day, using the master's technique, Bertie finds eight more balls, and only one of them is too badly scarred for use. And before the summer is out, the boy has amassed enough lost balls to purchase three golf clubs: a wood, an iron and a putter. His career, in other words, is launched.

● ● ●

It is autumn before Bertie sees the master again. He has teed off on the 14th link, his ball has hooked far to the left—over the fence, in fact, onto the bridle path. Right where the ball should be stands the master; only this time, there is a woman, not a dog, with him. She is a brunette and very pretty, although her ankles are a bit thick.

"Hey, kid," says the master, "where you been the last six weeks?"

"Playing golf, I guess," says Bertie

"Glad to hear it, kid. By the way, I want you to meet my wife, Gladys. Gladys, this is. . . what is your name, kid?"

"Bertie McKeon."

"Bertie McKeon," the master says to Gladys. "Remember that name. Bertie, I have a present for you, some things of no use to me anymore."

Bertie takes the old beach bag and opens it. It is full of golf balls, all of them shining white, round, perfect.

"There's that tough hole I was telling you about."

"Boy, I'll say my husband would be furious.
He's the greenskeeper."

"Last month he invented the wheel.
This month, who knows?"

it's a game that can drive you crazy—until you learn the one secret about golf worth knowing

humor By JAY CRONLEY one of the reasons this country is going to hell is because so many people play and watch golf. You could gas up all the four-door Lincolns on earth with what is spent each year on golf gloves.

The opinion that golf is a waste of time and energy and wood may sound like sour grapes, because I have been thrown out of a fancy-pants country club for behavior unbecoming a gentleman and because I have been struck by golf balls—most recently on the ass—more times than I can remember while playing public courses.

If you *have* to play golf, if it's in some rich aunt's will, it's best to start on the municipal courses and have your nickels and dimes (for ball markers) and C-notes (for dues), and then graduate to a country club where at least when somebody hits you on the ass, he will say he's sorry, and chances are he will be a doctor. About the only time a doctor shows up at a municipal course is after some poor blighter is hit on the skull by lightning. Whereas a shower might suspend play at a country club, you press onward at a public course, praying for golf-ball-sized hail, so you can practice some chips.

It's a long fall from paying your dues with a check to paying your dues with your rump, believe me.

I was standing behind the guy who was on the tee. I thought I was safe. You never know. The man took a practice swing beside his teed-up golf ball, and he had this strange recoil, like film was being run backward. He hit his teed-up golf ball with the back of his club on the recoil, sending a career drive into the left portion of my poor, unsuspecting ass.

"One," a member of our foursome said.

That was almost funny, but you never know about golf humor. Hubert Green once said something like, "Ninety-five percent of all putts you leave short don't go in," which is damn funny if he meant it that way.

I would like to think that the intense pain had something to do with the drive I hit, which hooked over a cart path, over a fence, over a road, into a herd of cows. But as of this writing, there are approximately 2450 reasons why a person hits a rotten shot, and more are being discovered every day.

As everybody who has had a pain in the ass knows, to compensate for this, you should move your left foot right and your right shoulder down and wear wolf teeth around your neck. Bob Toski, a famous teacher who gives lessons in magazines and on television, never shows you practical things, like how to drive when you can't feel your ass or how to hit one out of a trap when one of your partners is changing stations on his transistor radio.

But I was a slow learner and thought just this once God would take care of me and keep my golf ball in play. As my shot disappeared into the weeds and my partners marched down the fairway, I asked myself a very interesting question:

Why am I doing this?

There was no logical answer.

After all those years, I finally discovered the only secret of golf that makes perfect sense and works for everybody, and you don't even have to keep your head down to bring it off.

You're never too old to quit.

• • •

In 1980, there were 41 golf tournaments on network television, which proves it takes one to know one. I cannot imagine anybody but a hard-core golfer watching something like the Joe Garagiola Tucson Open.

My 12-year-old daughter doesn't even know who in the hell Joe Garagiola is.

She used to think he was Tim Conway.

Now she thinks he is Allen Funt.

She thinks Andy Williams is a goalie for the Cosmos.

Naming a golf tournament for a celebrity probably has some of the founding fathers spinning in their lateral hazards. Fortunately, other sports have resisted golf's tendency to try to put double knits on a dinosaur, or we would have things like the Steve Martin Indy 500 or the Marie Osmond Kentucky Derby; and as fortunately, Bob Hope has his golf tournament, the Desert Classic. In a way, there is a redeeming value in Hope's performance at his golf tournament; he acts like he's bigger than golf and talks during shots and wanders around, interviewing guys who couldn't break Jack Paar.

Sure, some of those things raise a lot of money for charity, but a change in the rules could make a few of the celebrity tournaments more tolerable. Since it seems that the only way some of the stars can get on television is by staging a golf tournament, there should be a rule stipulating that to qualify as a host, a "celebrity" has to have had a hit record within ten years, a prime-time television show or special within five years or a dog-food commercial within six months.

In 1980, golf tournaments were brought to us by Hope, Garagiola, Williams, Bing Crosby, Jackie Gleason, Glen Campbell, Danny Thomas and Sammy Davis Jr. The least they could do is change the Danny Thomas Memphis Classic to Marlo.

If ABC is, indeed, the leader in television sports, then maybe to a degree it's because of the old saw "What you don't know won't hurt you." ABC televised less golf in 1980 than the other networks. ABC carried the U.S. and British Opens, the PGA and Women's Open. CBS televised about everything that moved on the tour, including a few golfers—20 tournaments. (A CBS affiliate in New Orleans pre-empted the Crosby in 1979 to show Basil Rathbone in *The Hound of the Baskervilles,* so I guess there is some hope.)

In 1980, the Nielsen ratings for all golf telecasts took a dive for the fifth year in a row. One might guess that the reason golf got on television so much in the first place was because some network executive started showing off for his country-club pals, who owned things like box companies and freight lines, people who had never exchanged grips with Arnold Palmer.

It was obviously assumed that if somebody would watch the Masters, he would also watch the Tallahassee Open. The Masters is that tournament in Georgia where the winner gets a green jacket. The ceremony is so solemn, it looks like everybody is in the room to pick out a casket. The reason I always watch the Masters is to see if it's really true that a bird has never crapped on that golf course. The only reason I watched something like the Kemper Open was because there is a disgusting malfunction in us all, a crossed wire that makes something like a traffic accident interesting.

The networks have never subscribed to the hunch that absence makes the heart beat faster. The best strippers give you a leg and take it to the house. But with golf, it's assumed that, like with pro football, you can never get too much of a good thing.

There is, however, a difference between watching golf and watching other sports; team sports are more exciting. When a guy runs around end, any of 11 others can whack his ass, but a golf ball either goes in the hole or it doesn't. And whether the quarterback will pass or run is a much more interesting possibility to ponder than whether a golfer will hit a two or a three iron.

And even though the pro-basketball season is so long that some guys wrinkle as you watch, there is always the chance that a leaper will launch himself at the free-throw line and unleash a Second Coming of Christ Dunk that will uproot the backboard.

Baseball has reestablished itself as the national pastime because every now and then, there is an old-fashioned bloodletting where players throw bats and roll around on the ground in a big war, with arms and legs sticking out for the older players and managers to bite.

What golf's lousy ratings probably prove is that golf was never too exciting to watch and that any success it had on television in the past was because of guys like Palmer, who could have made flipping cards into a hat exciting.

Back when golf seemed fun, people like Tommy Bolt threw clubs and Walter Hagen would stay out all night and then play 18 holes of a tournament in a tuxedo.

Back when golf seemed fun, people like Tommy Bolt threw clubs and Walter Hagen would stay out all night and then play 18 holes of a tournament in a tuxedo.

Other sports build toward a championship, like the world series, but golf starts in January with the Hope and it concludes in December with the J.C. Penney Classic. There were 34 "classics" in 1980. The important tournaments are in the middle of the tour. So it doesn't really make a damn who does what, when the leading money winner is sometimes decided in the last few tournaments—

but accounting has never been a spectator sport.

The good thing about pro golf is that, unlike baseball, a person is paid according to his or her performance. Other pros are paid on the come and can bat .210 without having to eat root beer and peanuts for breakfast. But one of golf's charms—its pay-as-you-go system—is also one of the reasons the tour has become so stinking dull.

If you have to make a five-footer to eat, there is not time to smile.

When the announcers are more interesting than the event, you're in a hell of a shape. Jack Whitaker of CBS is the best there is at making you feel justified in watching a golf tournament instead of performing some meaningless task in the overall scheme of life, like taking a nap.

Quite frankly—and this is just between you and me—sometimes I don't understand what the fuck Jack Whitaker is talking about when he does one of those solos.

Talking about golf seems to bring out the poet in almost everybody; I have heard Jim McKay sound like he was trying to win a VFW essay contest.

I usually can't tell one announcer from another, except for Ben Wright, who has a British accent and describes shots as elegant or almost erotic.

Audrey Hepburn is elegant.

A golf shot is either crooked or straight.

The trend in television golf is to dispatch pros who don't make the cut in a tournament to report "live" from the fairway, with such valuable insight as: No, I can't hear you; it was heading for the trees; he is hitting a six iron, I think; or, I can't talk now, he's about to putt.

Golf has become so dull we're going to have to attack the problem at the core. Although the British have taught this country a lot about the sport, we never quite got the real lesson: You can lose money playing golf over there, just as you can playing the bases, hoops or football over here.

I know a bookie who rehandicaps dull pro-football games at the half, so if it's 28-zip at intermission, there's still a reason to stay tuned. They give you odds on baseball, like if Guidry is going for the Yankees at home against some yokel, you might have to bet $100 to win $40.

And there is nothing like an over/under number to jazz up a Pistons-Bulls basketball game. The over/under number is the predicted number of total points both teams will score. Some dog can be behind 35 and your bet can still be decided on a last-second Nut-Cracker Slam Dunk.

My bookie says the paperwork would be unbelievable if he tried to handicap golf. His computer might short out. But you give me some "young lion" like Artie McNickle at 100-1 and I'll believe Jack Whitaker if he suggests golf is bigger than both of us, and I'll listen if Jim McKay tries to rhyme Augusta with something.

The future of golf on television is in the hands of this country's bookies.

• • •

But watching golf on TV is one thing. Trying to watch a golf tournament in person is like trying to cover a war on foot. It's supposed to be a social event, until you have to go to the bathroom; then it's every person for him- or herself. I have been purposely gouged in the back by rich people trying to weasel into the remote john line.

The only reason to watch a golf tournament in person is to look at the girls wearing haltertops and shorts or to get some sun; but if you try that, they'll throw your ass out, which is still better than getting your ass hit.

I attended the U.S. Open in Tulsa in 1977 because there was nothing else to do and because that was the year word reached us that going braless was good for your circulation. That was also the year the popular style in shorts was little more than two pockets taped to one's fanny.

It was unbelievable.

The players, though, looked like a convention of business majors. I hear some of the old Opens were exciting—like in 1934, when Bobby Cruickshank hit a great shot, threw his club into the air and was knocked unconscious.

My fondest memory of the 1977 Open was when a redhead asked if I was Morris Hatalsky, to which I answered no, because all she wanted was an autograph. I hear the groupies have moved on to soccer.

At the Open, I located a place on a hill and was promptly told by one of the marshals that I had to wear a shirt. Marshals at a golf tournament are usually club members who work without pay, which sounds very noble at face value. Except that after you have met a few of those clowns, it becomes apparent that getting to wear a little helmet and uniform is reward enough. There is nothing like a marshal's badge to turn some meek 19-handicapper into a tough guy. The one in charge of the gallery rope near where I was sunbathing suggested that because portions of that hole would be on national television, we didn't want to suggest to the rest of the world that we just fell off the enchilada truck, did we?

I told the little punk that not only would I keep my shirt off but when J.C. Snead came past, I might fizz a beer on him. The marshal got on his walkie-talkie and called for a backup unit to come out and hose me off with some Grey Flannel by Geoffrey Beene.

It's fun to tease the marshals by rattling ice or by sneezing, both of which are grounds for being hung by the feet at the clubhouse. You can get away with a scratch out there on the fairway, but if you by God have a heart attack at the green, you had better fall away from the putting surface, so as not to disturb somebody like Fuzzy Zoeller.

He won the Masters.

A popular way to watch a tournament in person is to follow some golfer 18 holes, which is not much fun, because to see anything, you have to be 6'10" or follow a bum. Or you can follow somebody like Tom Watson and stand in five-deep rows and ask the person in front, "What's he doing now?" and wait for the answer, "Nothing," to be passed back.

Tom Watson is a hell of a golfer, but he sure could use a choreographer. Watching him shoot 66 is like watching the President sign a bill. You have a hunch he's doing the right thing, but it's sort of impersonal.

At the Open in 1977, I saw Jack Nicklaus' hair and the top of his putter.

I guess there is an argument to be made for going early and nailing down a seat at a green. I did that once and was there so early I had to go to the bathroom before the first foursome arrived, and I watched the rest of the tournament from atop a portable outhouse. After sitting at a green an hour or so, you are ready for somebody to take a vote; it's like a board meeting. If some hack is standing over a putt and your stomach growls, the golfer is liable to stand up, back off and scowl at you contemptuously, as though you had just crawled out from under a beer can.

Tennis is stuffy enough, but at least when you are expected to be quiet, something is going on; with golf, if you clear your throat while somebody is in the preparatory stages of thinking about a putt, well, that breaks down a golfer's concentration and it's your fault if he chokes on a two-footer.

Chekhov wrote with screaming children under foot, and Johnny Unitas completed many intricate passes as guys threatened to poke his eyeballs out, and Rick Barry could make a free throw with the

Rockettes on either side of the free-throw line.

But golf is one of the few sports streakers have avoided. Any woman running bare-breasted across a green would probably be shot or, worse, ignored.

• • •

I joined a country club because it was the only place I could get a decent cheeseburger, and also because I was out of my mind: just married and trying to impress a wife. It just shows how dumb a game golf can be; when the divorce came, too much golf was a factor.

There are many fallacies about golf, but none so universally accepted as the one that a lot of business deals are made on the golf course. I made as many business deals on the golf course in three years of country-club membership as I did in 15 minutes of shooting baskets at the YMCA: none.

Golf is a tax loophole that even I could drive a three wood through. You are permitted to write off that percentage of dues and things that apply to business, monkey or otherwise.

The country club reinforces golf's snob appeal.

Poor slobs need not apply.

Although money might talk at a municipal course, where ten dollars will get you ten minutes off a starting time, money snores at the average country club. I used to play golf with guys who would bet $100 on how many little dents were on a golf ball. I was the one they paid five dollars to, to count the dents.

Although golf is thought to be a gentleman's game, it promotes cheating through the handicapping system. The worse you play, the higher your handicap is, which permits you to rob honest guys like me blind. I once played nine holes with a man who shot 54 and beat me out of some lettuce. That's fun?

It is also said that scenery is a pleasurable aspect of golf; all the years I played, I never saw a damn thing. I played from inside the scenery.

And quite a few people told me I should join the club because golf was good exercise. I have since learned that it is possible to play 18 holes without burning off much more than 75 calories, that many only if you are attacked by bees.

"All golf does is spoil a good walk," says Dr. Edward St. Mary, the medical consultant to the Miami Dolphins. When you ride a cart, you burn off about 222 calories an hour, if you turn a lot. If you ride a cart, you get more exercise spitting watermelon seeds.

They tossed me out of the country club the day I went berserk

during a tournament and used the Lord's name in vain, ripped my shirt off and rolled around in a trap like a mad dog. I was playing against a little man who could pee about as far as he could hit a drive.

The man I played in the tournament shall remain nameless, because, for all I know, he could melt down his ball markers and hire some cruncher to feed me to the perch.

I had been known to blast a golf ball. I once drove one from the tenth tee to the tenth green at Southern Hills in Tulsa, which has never been done or will be done again. I hit the ball so hard it about cried. It flew over about 100 trees and went over a housing addition, but hooked back onto the field of combat and rolled to the green. Then I four-putted, so the drive didn't make much of a damn, did it?

> *They tossed me out of the club the day I went berserk during a tournament and used the Lord's name in vain, ripped my shirt off and rolled around in a trap like a mad dog.*

On a par five during my last tournament, I pounded two shots into a trap by the green. My partner crept down the fairway, a bit at a time, like he was playing tiddlywinks. It was dangerously windy that day and a limb had blown across the far edge of the trap. My golf ball was about 30 yards from the limb, which wasn't in the trap, it was over the edge. So, like any normal person, I picked up the limb and carried it off.

My opponent called the hole on me. It is illegal to remove an object from in or over a trap, even if it's a dead body.

It took my opponent about seven shots to reach the green, but all that mattered was that I had broken a rule of golf and, as he joyfully explained to me, we had to protect the integrity of the game.

I never understood all the rules. (There is one, I think, that says if you hit a shot and a water moccasin eats your golf ball before it stops rolling, you have to swing the son of a bitch counterclockwise around your head six times; then, if the snake doesn't spit out the ball, you can bash its brains out on a ball washer, though one no nearer the hole.)

I stomped off the course without settling various tabs, so they put a lawyer on my trail. I got a loan and squared things.

One of the things I owed for was lessons. I had taken hundreds of dollars' worth of lessons. They had put me on videotape machines and looked at the evidence and said I had basically a horse-shit swing, which I knew in the first place.

I had also bought hundreds of dollars' worth of clothing and gear from the pro shops. They come out with some new shaft, something like a kangaroo-bone driver, every couple of years. Pros like Johnny Miller get endorsement deals with companies like Sears. Every time I tried to look like Johnny Miller, all I had the desire to do was sell refrigerators.

I had even tried to comprehend lessons from magazines, where drawings of golfers had arrows around their heads and between their legs.

But the only thing I ever learned from belonging to a country club was how to drink a bloody Mary while walking.

• • •

It's hard to quit anything cold turkey; so after being struck on the ass, after being booted out of the club, I played one more round of golf with the vice-president of a big company. The only thing that brought me out of retirement this last time was hatred—I wanted this guy, bad.

He was real phony and kept telling me how Watson would play this shot and Trevino that one. But I had him by his Titleists.

He kept doubling his bets, and going to the 17th hole, there was the distinct possibility that I would be moving into my opponent's house that night.

The reason I was playing so well was because I had had about five beers and hadn't swung a golf club in four years. Golf is one of the few sports you can play all right drunk.

He weaseled one off the tee that flew into some bulrushes, and he blamed it on a cloud. I clothes-lined one that hooked, sliced, knuckled and came to rest in the middle of the goddamn fairway.

From where my golf ball was, I could have underhanded it onto the green, but as I stood there, basking in the sun and glory, thinking maybe I had been wrong about the value of golf, my opponent off to the right said, "I found it, it's one foot in bounds!"

"Stop that, you cheating bastard!" I yelled.

A ball flew out of the weeds and landed on the green.

This character ripped his glove off, like he had just done a heart bypass, and he drove his cart to the green.

I lost the 17th and 18th holes and had to pay this rat $20.

I blasted my last shot over the clubhouse.

PLAYBOY'S PARTY JOKES

GOLF DIDN'T COME NATURALLY to the housewife who was taking up the game, and the basic problem seemed to be a defective grip. "I'm afraid this may be putting it crudely, Mrs. Wallingford," said the frustrated teaching pro, "but I suggest you take hold of the club as you would your husband's erect organ."

The woman made the adjustment, swung the club and drove the ball 200 yards straight down the fairway. "Great shot!" exclaimed the astonished pro. "Now I suggest you take the club out of your mouth and try using it with your hands."

• • •

WHEN HE COULD squeeze in the time, the Pope made arrangements to play nine holes of golf. At the seventh hole, a 175-yard par-three to an island green, he prudently decided to tee up an old ball. Suddenly, a thunderous voice boomed from above, "Tee up a new ball."

The pontiff dutifully bent down and replaced the old ball with a new one. Once again, a thunderous voice boomed, "Now step back and take a few practice swings."

The Pope stepped back and practiced his swing. Several minutes passed, then he heard a sigh and the voice from above intoned, "OK, tee up the old ball."

"Aren't you going to repair your ball marks?"

"Did I wake you?"

*"Of course we have to do it this way. How else can I see if
you're bringing the right muscles into play?"*

PLAYBOY'S PARTY JOKES

THE GOLFER confidently eyed the next hole and remarked to his caddy: "This should be good for a long drive and a putt." His swing, however, hit the sod and pushed the ball only a few feet.

"Now," said the caddy, "for a hell of a putt."

"Don't laugh, yesterday, he was five under par on the back nine!"

fiction **By KEVIN COOK**

LEE AND ME AT THE OPEN

I GOT UP that morning feeling pretty good. Pretty loose, ready to go all the way around Pebble Beach one more time without losing my concentration. Sports are concentration as much as anything else. Any professional athlete will tell you that the competition is a lot more mental than physical when you get to a professional level. In my case, I guess you'd have to say it was almost all mental.

I think my varied background is what made my whole golf career possible. The acting came first, from high school right up

remember me, orval greene,
golf's greene machine?
remember that last round
at pebble beach?
here's what really happened

through college. Then I decided there was more security in software. By software, I don't mean Tupperware; I mean computer software—all the advanced new programs for the advanced new computers. I knew that was where the future was, and that was what finally made me the most loved and famous and awesome golfer of all time. And modest, too. I'm still modest, but now I've got real good reasons to be.

> *I knew that was where the future was, and that was what finally made me the most loved and famous and awesome golfer of all time.*

I was the most loved and famous and awesome for a while, anyway. For a while, they said Nicklaus was a decent club player compared with me. Jones was a high school hacker and everybody else, from Hogan to Watson, never should have left the Putt-Putt. It's damn sure nobody else ever shot 260 to win the Masters by 23 strokes. Dan Jenkins from *Sports Illustrated* was so star-struck, he used to knock over a Jack Daniel's bottle every time I came into the clubhouse. They were all like that.

Not anymore, damn 'em. Now they call my career "meteoric," with the emphasis on when I hit the ground.

Anyway, the guys at *Golf Magazine* called me up to see if I'd write a story on that last round at Pebble Beach. You'll notice they didn't ask for a series of stories, even though I was the biggest thing that ever happened to the game. Nowadays, most people want to forget about me. The blazer guys especially want to forget about me— Frank Hannigan and Beman and the rest of them. You'd think I was a baboon with the clap the way they stay away from me.

Golf didn't ask me to be on its advisory staff, either. Well, that's OK. I turned them down before, when I was hot. Who wants to sit around a table with Johnny Miller and Tom Weiskopf and three other guys who look just like Jerry McGee? *All* the young ones look like Jerry McGee. Must be their Amana hats.

No, *Golf* doesn't want me on its Jerry McGee staff now, but that's OK with me. I guess Weiskopf's off it now, anyway. I think he bogeyed his first article, withdrew and went home. Ha-ha. Little Tom Weiskopf joke there.

Used to be, magazines had to run after me just to get a quote to put in their book, and then they'd put my name on the cover, like I had a whole article inside or something. "ORVAL GREENE ON BUNKER PLAY," the cover would say, when all they had inside was something I said coming off the course, like "I don't care if they fill up all the traps with Jell-O. I'm never in 'em."

So, looks like I've got this article to write. Might as well get on it—I need the money. Alimony. You probably remember Billie Lou. They had a whole issue of *People* about us when we got married under the press tent at the '82 Open. Maybe some of you guys remember her as the Playmate of the Year a few years ago. I think she's Warren Beatty's playmate now.

Like I said, I felt pretty loose that Sunday morning. Knew I could keep it going and make it look good. The program called for me to hit a tree on two and make a bogey, then get it back with a spectacular bird from the trap on three. It was a good program, and I was smiling and joking around with the writers while I knocked back a chicken-fried steak and three eggs for breakfast.

Then I went out to the putting green and dropped a few balls. I played Spalding Dots, even though Wilson made a ball called the Greene Champion, which was a solid piece of white stuff—kind of like a round tooth. I knew it was going to be a great day. I sniffed the sea breeze. I didn't know then that I was about to take seven on the Par Five of Life.

• • •

Let me tell you how I worked the whole thing out. A buddy of mine at Kansas Instruments helped me put together a microcomputer small enough to fit in a golf ball. We did it as a demonstration—to show the boss we could get a pretty sophisticated machine down to that size. It made for a great demonstration: "Look here, J.B., we've got a Titleist X-out here with all the knowledge of the Library of Congress inside."

It didn't go much further than that. There's not much call for smart golf balls in the Business Office of Tomorrow. The boss gave us a pat on the back and said maybe we could get the thing to make a hole in one every time, har-de-har.

Well, he was close.

If I had the layout of a golf course, I figured, I could lay out the yardage in two dimensions and feed the perfect placement of each shot into the memory of the little computer. Then it would just be a matter of setting all the perfect placements in order, so the ball *would* go into the fairway from the tee, then go to the next programmed spot, in the right sequence. It took about a month of

PLAYBOY'S PARTY JOKES

*H*ARRY AND *F*RED were playing money golf, 10 bucks a hole. After the first, Harry asked Fred how many strokes he had taken. Fred answered five.

"I was home in four," said Harry smiling, "so that's my hole."

When they finished the second, Harry asked the same question.

"Wait a minute," Fred objected. "It's my turn to ask first."

• • •

"I HATE TO GO GOLFING with any of the executives from my own agency," complained the advertising president, while relaxing with his fourth scotch and soda at the clubhouse bar. "Every time I yell 'Fore' they chime in with '. . . he's a jolly good fellow!'"

• • •

"I WON'T SAY I'm getting old," the aging duffer told his golfing partner, "but lately my sex drive's turned into a putt."

"I don't like the looks of this—it could be the
end of sex as we know it."

tinkering before I had a ball that knew where to go for every shot in a whole round of golf.

The problem was that the ball didn't know how to get there. If you hit it from the tee with an inside-out swing, the baby would just hook right into the bushes, knowing all along that it ought to be in the middle of the fairway 290 yards out. The problem was propulsion. It took a while, but I solved it.

Now, they're not paying me near enough to get me to let the secret out, but I will tell you one thing. The reason I always used the Spalding Dot, when all the other pros played Pro-Staffs and Titleists and Tourneys, was the key. You know that little black spot on the dot? Well, if you ever took a magnifying glass to my ball, you'd see it should really have been called a Spalding Exhaust Pipe. Clever, huh? So, I had me a sophisticated little computer with an automatic-guidance system and propulsion from the oxygenation of hydrogen fuel (which was in the liquid center). I was ready to take on the tour.

It worked pretty well, but some of the bugs weren't worked out right at the start. They gave me a few scares, like the time in the Byron Nelson when I hit a drive that went about 700 yards—"Hot damn! That wind in Texas shore do kick up, don't it?"—but I got them all straightened out and settled down to the business of becoming the most loved and awesome and all that stuff golfer.

You think it'd be really hard to get a computer in a golf ball? Then you just don't understand how advanced our technology is, pal. All I had to do was program the thing to go to its preordained spot every time it took a hard jolt. That way, it wouldn't take off like a rocket when I tried to putt. Since the sequence of 36–40 shots was all locked in the night before, when I sat down in the hotel with a layout of the course, nothing could go wrong.

I was on my own on the greens, of course, but then I hardly ever fixed it so I'd be more than ten feet away. If I three-putted, so what? I'd have five or six tap-in birdies a day, anyway, and I could always put in a few flag-biters the next day, if I missed too many.

The toughest thing was to make it *look* convincing. If you're going to beat Tom Watson by 15 strokes in the Crosby, you damn well better not look like Andy Williams when you swing or somebody's going to suspect something. I had played in college (number-two man at Kansas State in a down year), and I worked with video tapes of Sam Snead's swing for three months until our swings started to look quite a bit alike. So, then, all I had to do was look pretty reasonable out there and I could start practicing my wave to the crowd.

Guess you're probably ready to hear about that last day at Pebble Beach by now.

"*Maybe I can chip out of this stuff, and then get home with a three iron. . . but even if I carry the water hazard and the sand traps, I'm still staring at a double bogey. Wanna fuck?*"

I was paired with Trevino and with Danny Sterling, the kid from Wake Forest who would wind up low amateur. They both put their tee shots on one right down the pipe, but nobody really cared, of course. I was the hot ticket, and the Greene Goblins were lined up ten deep in the gallery. I had a nine-stroke lead, and the program was for a straight, dead-solid-perfect drive off the first tee.

It took off like an ICBM, about six feet off the ground the first 50 yards. Then it started to rise and didn't come down until the gasps did and I was a good 60 yards farther out than the other two guys.

The ball was working like a charm. I could have shot 63 on a good day, but the putts weren't falling.

I heard Ben Wright intone "Dear God. . ." into his ABC microphone and headed down the fairway the way you would if you'd just hit a 310-yard drive off the first tee on the last day of the Open.

Things went fine all day long. Made a couple of bogeys on eight and nine, just to keep the folks by their TVs, while Lee was starting to get real hot. I wasn't worried, though. Does General Motors worry if Schwinn sells a few extra bikes?

Lee and I were the only red numbers on the board as we came to the turn. I was 11 under and he was minus four. Crenshaw was even (Wright insisted he was "level"). Ben is the best damn second-and-third-place finisher in the majors the world will ever know.

The ball was working like a charm. I could have shot 63 on a good day, but the putts weren't falling. Maybe you remember that nobody ever called me a great putter, because I was actually just a club player out there with the guys on the tour. So I always missed my share of four-footers. Anyway, I still had four strokes on Lee, coming to 16. Everybody else was out of it by then. It was ticking me off a little that Lee was staying so close—I had at least ten strokes on the rest of the field. He kept cracking jokes and making birdies, but I knew my birdie-birdie-birdie finish was coming up, so the old Mex would need an eagle and two holes in one to catch me. I wasn't too worried.

Sterling hit first, at 16. He'd just made birdie to bring him back to eight over for the day. The low ams usually don't shoot the lights out on the last day, playing late with their heroes, and I could tell the kid idolized the hell out of me. I hit next—a real thunderball, down the left side. We had to wait for Lee to finish telling a joke before he hit: "What's the difference between a nymphomaniac, a prostitute and a housewife? A nymphomaniac says, 'Is it over?' A prostitute says, 'It's over' and a housewife says, 'I think I'll paint the ceiling yellow.'"

Lee said his wife would get on him pretty good for that one, then he hit a high fade out into the middle and followed me into the fairway.

I waited for him to hit. He took a six iron and put it into the trap on the left. He looked over at me and smiled and said, "Well, amigo, unless you start taking sevens, this is about over, isn't it?"

Sterling hit a six about 40 yards over the green and nearly died of embarrassment.

I got to my ball and looked it over, took an eight and concentrated hard on making my swing look like Sam's. I knew that if I slipped and still hit the ball or even if I forgot which way the green was and faced the tee and hit it that way, the ball would head straight for the heart of the green. It was important to keep up appearances.

Lee moseyed over and looked at my ball.

"How come you play a Dot?" he said.

"I like 'em."

"No click. Everybody else plays Pro-Staffs."

"Well, they tend to explode when I hit 'em." I thought I might as well lay it on thick.

He looked down at my ball. "Looks like that one already did."

"What?"

"The stuffings are coming out."

He was right. I tried to keep my eyes from bugging out of my head. I'd put a smile in the ball somewhere along the line.

"You got a jolly little golf ball," Lee said.

"Yeah. Must have skulled one somewhere."

"It's even got teeth."

"Huh?"

"The smile's even got teeth."

My little chips and microprocessors were trying to slip out through the smile.

"Well, I better hit it before it gets any worse."

I put a desperate Gerald Ford swing on it, and the ball acted like a missile with its guidance center falling out the bottom. It fluttered and pushed a little black smoke out the exhaust pipe and hit about 60 feet past the pin. Still, the programming held true and the ball backed up 56 feet, until it was right next to the pin.

Lee looked a little suspicious by this time. "A lot of bite on that ball," he said.

I gave him a queasy grin. "Must have been the teeth, I guess." As I hustled up to the green, the crowd was giving me a standing ovation.

I was just reaching down to replace my ball with an intact back-up ball when one of the blazer guys stopped me and asked to take a look. He was the tournament director.

He took it out of my hand and rubbed it on his blazer. Some of the chips were starting to fall out now. He squeezed and sparks popped out of the smile.

The tournament director looked at me and said, "I don't think this is a regulation ball."

I said, "Damn that Spalding company! I should have been playing Pro-Staffs all along, just like Lee said."

"We'll have to take them all and examine them. I'll have someone bring you a dozen new balls." He turned and got in his cart.

"Wait a minute!" I yelled. "You can't just take my balls!"

"What is this material on the inside of the ball?"

"How do I know? Maybe it's a bomb. Maybe somebody's trying to kill me."

As he zipped away through the gallery, he said, "We'll find out."

I stood there and watched the blazer chug away with my career in his pocket. A kid brought me a dozen regular Spalding Dots, helped me open a boat and take one out, then pushed me in the direction of the green. The crowd crunched in around me. My caddy handed me my putter and said, "Hey, you been cheatin', man?" All in all, it was a bad moment.

Lee came over and said he was sorry if he'd caused me any trouble. He mumbled something like, "Muchachas siesta por favor, amigo, tostada burrito yoyo bolos," which he translated as, "You never stop trying as long as you've got the balls."

I was an 11 handicapper with good form and an ordinary golf ball. I had two holes to play and a four-stroke lead. My brains were trying to slide out through the smile in my face.

Just then, I realized I had found my way into every golfer's dream. There I was, standing over a putt for a five-stroke lead in the last round in the U.S. Open, looking across the green at Lee Trevino, who had just saved par to stay close. Millions of people were watching on TV.

I stood over the putt and looked at the hole, a long four feet away, and watched my hands shake. Then, over a monitor somewhere, I heard Jim McKay say, "And now Orval Greene, the Greene

"Listen, honey, I know you are worried about your putting,
but I have an awful lot of laundry to finish."

81

Machine, bids to close the door on Trevino and take his place in the lore of this great game. . ." and I knew I couldn't let down every duffer who ever dreamed this dream.

I glared at the hole, like Nicklaus, and gripped my putter and held on until it stopped shaking. I put it behind the ball and waited for minutes, and then I drew the blade back and brought it through. I made it.

The crowd went nuts. Lee looked a little surprised, but he came over and patted me on the back. We went to 17, the par three. I had a five-stroke lead with two to play. I had the honor.

• • •

People have asked me ever since why I didn't just hang it up right then, knowing the blazers were going to find out about the ball and kick me out on my rear.

Did you ever think what you'd do if sometime you woke up and you were standing on the stage at the Met, with 200 people all dressed up behind you and a full house in front of you, and you were wearing a big helmet with horns? Well, you'd sing, wouldn't you?

I stood over the ball on the 17th tee and glared again, just like Nicklaus. I took a smooth practice swing and a deep breath, and then hit a worm burner off the tee. It bounced down over the ladies' tee and into the rough out in front of me and stopped a good 75 yards short of the green. The ball just sat there, dead, like a lump. It was a real ball, all right.

Sterling stuck a three about 12 feet from the flag, and then Lee threw in a two iron even closer.

I got to my ball and hit a wedge into the trap at the back left of the green. Didn't have to wait for anybody—I was still away. My caddy started running up toward the green, embarrassed to be connected with my last two shots.

My bunker shot just made it out onto the edge of the green. I was still away. I got the ball down in two, since my first putt rifled into the back of the hole and only went six inches by. Lee and the kid both made their birdie putts, and my lead on Lee was two strokes.

The 18th at Pebble Beach is that famous par five that winds its way around the Pacific. The Pacific is that famous ocean that drinks up balls that wind the wrong way on the 18th. The other two guys hit big drives down the left side, flirting with the water. My driver was shaking in my hand like an electric eel, but I held it down and popped one about 175 yards from the tee, out into the right rough.

Then I rushed out and hacked at a three wood. That only went 100 yards.

I was still about 275 yards from the green. I could have taken a fairway wood and tried to get it close to the front, but I decided on a two iron. If Lee made par (and anybody who birdies the 18th at Pebble on the last day of the Open deserves to win and be made king besides), then a bogey would still win for me.

I turned to my caddy with my teeth clenched. "Gimme a two iron. I'm going to win this thing."

He said, "I can't understand you when you got your mouth closed."

"A two! I want a two!"

He handed it over, and I waggled a little. It was quiet everywhere in the world.

I backed away, waggled again. I saw Ben Hogan in my mind, and Palmer charging, and Player and Miller on the last day at Oakmont, and Trevino at Merion and Nicklaus everywhere. I nailed that two, and it took off low and then rose and didn't come down again until it was just 20 yards short of the green.

The crowd went wild, and I grinned right in the face of Frank Hannigan and all the other blazers who wanted to do me in.

• • •

Well, you know how it all wound up. Lee made that beautiful eight-footer for his par, and I needed a downhill four-footer with a little left break on it for a one-stroke win.

It was just a little one, the kind you'd call a gimme if you were playing with your pals on Sunday morning. But they don't have gimmes in the Open.

I looked at it for a good five minutes, just standing there glaring at the black dot on the ball—that little black spot of paint with no exhaust pipe in it. I looked at it some more, and still the ball didn't move.

Lee said, "Winter's coming, *amigo*."

Wright whispered, "And it appears that at last, the great man is going to strike his tiny spheroid, and will it find its way into that marvelous pit or will it stay, like a rebellious child, at the entrance and refuse to go in?"

My caddy whispered in my ear, "You better make it, honkie."

Like I said, it was downhill, so I just started it rolling.

It seemed to roll forever before it got in the neighborhood of the hole, picking up speed all the time.

It started its break late and just caught the right lip and spun all the way around, until it was on the right lip again and I was looking at that black dot on the ball as it hovered on the last blade of grass between it and the bottom of the cup.

• • •

The crowd went wild, and I grinned right in the face of Frank Hannigan and all the other blazers who wanted to do me in.

You probably remember the whole scene. Lee and I both fainted dead away, and the kid Sterling fell to the green in imitation of us. We looked like the end of *Hamlet,* the three of us there flat on the green, our putters lying next to us like swords.

The ball wavered.

The blazers clustered around the back of the green, waving their arms like chickens. They were trying to decide which one of us should be revived first. They decided on Lee, since he had honors on the hole.

The TV guys were getting excited, shouting into their microphones, showing close-ups of us sprawled on the green, with insets of the ball, teetering.

Then the fans just lost control and broke through the ropes and came pouring out around us. And that, of course, jarred the ground, and the ball fell in.

When they put smelling salts under my nose and brought me around, they had my trophy and my permanent suspension waiting at a red-and-white-striped table in front of the clubhouse, and that was the end of my brilliant career.

• • •

So, it was fun while it lasted, even if they do treat me like a doggy scooper now.

I spend most of my time now watching videotapes of Garo Yepremian. You know, a football is a lot bigger than a golf ball, and I'm working on a real smart one.

I know no NFL club is going to want to give me a tryout, but maybe I can force their hand.

Last week, I kicked a field goal at the Rams game. From section 24, row UU, seat 31.

"The greens committee is certainly
going to hear about this!"

*"Oh, for Pete's sake, Ruth—why can't you just accept being a
golf widow the way other women do?!"*

87

PLAYBOY'S PARTY JOKES

"*H*OW ABOUT that shapely new female pro?" leered a regular of the golf club.

"It's a waste of time," advised a fellow member.

"How do you know?"

"I've already gotten out of bounds with her and learned she's an unpliable lay."

• • •

*A*N INNER-CITY youngster who had never seen a game of golf was working as a gas-station attendant when a top-of-the-line Cadillac rolled in. While the driver left the vehicle to make a phone call, the boy examined the car hungrily and found some golf tees on top of the dashboard. "What are those things for, mister?" he asked as the man returned.

"They're to put my balls on when I'm driving," was the reply.

"Gee," sighed the boy, "those Caddie people sure think of everything!"

"Of course we let them play through."

THE DAY ARNOLD PALMER
WAS BLACKBALLED
AT THE FAIRWOOD
GOLF AND TENNIS CLUB
humor **By PETER ANDREWS**

Harry! A bourbon and water. And this time don't drown it . . . Well, you fellows can do whatever you want to . . . I don't pretend to be the only man on the Greens Committee, but if you ask me, I'd ban every single one of these touring professionals from Fairwood right now. Who thought up this ridiculous idea of a two-ball tourney with professionals, anyway? I mean, that pro-am tournament Bing Crosby runs at Pebble Beach really cuts it thin enough. But my God! When you set up a tournament where a pro and an amateur actually play side by side and take alternate shots at the same ball, then, for my money, you come pretty close to ruining the whole spirit of the game. Are we really sure that is the sort of thing we want for Fairwood? Are we? I mean, that is a game that calls for the kind of teamwork you can't expect when you harness a sportsman to a professional. One thing I do know— Arnold Palmer will never be allowed inside this club again as long as there is a breath left in my body. . . .

Who did you play with today, Ralph?. . . . Billy Casper! Now, I hear he's a real gentleman. But fellow, you can have this Palmer.

Did you hear about him stalking off the course in the middle of the round today?. . . . Incredible!. . . . Of course I know what happened. . . . Listen . . . I was the one who had drawn him as a partner. . . . We played together and I saw the whole thing.

Palmer and I were paired with this professional, Phil Rodgers, and the other amateur member was George Wilson. I don't know why Wilson was put in with us. Frankly, if it comes to that, I don't know what Wilson is doing in this club at all.

Who did you play with today, Ralph? . . . Billy Casper! Now, I hear he's a real gentleman. But fellow, you can have this Palmer.

He's so damned vain about that four handicap of his. Never actually mentions it right out, of course. He's too smart for that. But he has that smug air about him when he swings that lets you know he thinks he's better than you are. If there's one thing that has no place on a golf course, it's that kind of attitude. No place at all.

Anyway, Palmer and I were first off and, more as a courtesy to a guest than anything else, I gave him first shot. Right away I was glad I did, because I was able to give him some help. . . . Listen, I don't care what kind of professional you are, or where you've played before, there is something about standing up there on the first tee of the Fairwood Golf and Tennis Club that tightens the nerves. Palmer must have felt it, too, because I noticed that instead of that smooth, fluid backswing you need, there was a little pause—no, it seemed more like a hitch—right at the top of his backswing. I think he might have pulled himself off his stance just a little and was try-ing to get back together. Anyway, he hit the ball kind of fat. He got lucky, though, and just managed to clear the downhill slope of the fairway and pick up enough roll to get out about 285 yards. . . . I know, I know. It was a long drive. . . . But you know as well as I do that sooner or later Fairwood punishes the sloppy hitter. And today, the way they have absolutely ruined the course with a lot of tricks to let the pros show off their muscles, I knew we weren't always going to be so lucky. So on our way down to the ball I told him, in a very friendly way, about that hitch. When I said it, he looked kind of surprised. You know, he probably hadn't noticed it himself. You can get that way if you let yourself get all wrapped up in your own game and don't think about anyone else. . . . Listen, I read all the time about the pros getting into trouble and having to go and get straightened out. No one is so good at this game that he can't use a little help. Anyway, Palmer just said, "Thanks for the tip, pal," and walked on down the fairway.

But, you know, a lot of these professional golfers haven't had too much education and don't know any better, so I let it pass as his way of trying to be friendly with me.

Now, you know me. I didn't expect him to call me Dr. Martinson all the time, but I can't say I liked that "pal" stuff too much. Maybe spending 18 years building up a gynecology practice may not seem like a whole lot to him, but it's damned important to me. But, you know, a lot of these professional golfers haven't had too much education and don't know any better, so I let it pass as his way of trying to be friendly with me.

Anyway, our ball was about 145 yards from the green and I laid into it with my brassie pretty good—but at the last minute the wind got ahold of it and the ball just trickled out of bounds on the right.

I didn't really mind the first hole, though. As long as I am hitting the ball well, I know that the score will take care of itself. And, besides, I noticed that since I pointed out that hitch to him, Palmer was hitting good, too. I had to keep reminding him, though. . . . You know how easy it is to forget something new the first few times around. . . . Anyway, he kept nodding and told me he thought he had the hang of it now.

Golf is a game of inches. There's no question about that. And it was on the fourth hole where just a few inches meant the difference. I don't have to tell you about that fourth—536 yards of sheer murder. Well, I smacked a drive. I mean, I really smacked a drive—a

"The tests show it's your lungs. You're breathing too much sand."

slow-rising, quail-high job—but it just barely caught the tips of those bushes around the water hazard about 25 yards in front of the tee, or it would have really flown. I had some tough luck and the ball dropped in the saw-grass and was down there pretty good. Palmer got out, but he seemed to hit it sort of up and a little high instead of snapping it out there the way he should have. I told him when you're in that saw grass, you've got to really flatten out that swing and punch it out if you want to get any distance. Even though he got some wind behind him, we were still about 250 yards from home.

I had a lot of yardage to make up from where he left me, so I laid a spoon right where I wanted it in the light rough on the right side. That gave him a real good 130-yard control shot to the green over the roadway through the gap between that clump of spruce and the soft-drink shack over by the 11th tee. But, like a lot of these pros, Palmer doesn't know what to do unless he's got an absolutely open shot to the green. He let those low-lying weeping-willow branches buffalo him. I told him not to worry. I told him it was just like the saw-grass shot. I told him to take a three iron and slap one through the break in the trees. If you hit one just right with a little fade, it can fly those traps and settle on the green. I told him not to be afraid of it. . . . I told him to just choke up on the three iron and punch it right up there.

You know, the one single quality that stands out most about professional athletes is their almost complete lack of manners. All the time I was getting Palmer set for the shot, this Rodgers fellow was laughing at him. I mean it. Rodgers was actually laughing at him just because Palmer had this delicate shot. You know how a needler can take all the fun out of a round. But I guess all Rodgers wanted to do was win, no matter how. Because, as a matter of fact, he kept it up the whole round. Not even an open, man's laugh either, but one of those behind-the-hand sniggers where you pretend you're trying to hold it back but let everyone hear it anyway. I could see all that laughing was getting under Palmer's skin, because he wasn't even thinking. He must have used the wrong club—I think it was an eight or something—and tried to power it over the trees. That's no way to play that shot. I guess he skulled it or something. Anyway, it stopped about 20 feet in back of the green on the downhill side from where it was absolutely impossible for me to steer my wedge away from the trap. Palmer got out but couldn't put it any closer to the hole than about five feet. He must save his good shots for television. I had to save the score by laying an approach putt stony to the pin for Palmer to sink.

I could see that Palmer was off his feed, but we were just going to have to pull up our socks and get moving if we wanted to turn the corner in any kind of shape. It wasn't going to be any cinch, because he was really letting his bad play get his goat. I tried to draw him out in conversation, but he hardly said a word. Although I noticed that once he did take Rodgers aside and started nodding and talking real seriously. Probably told him to stop that laughing stuff. God knows, if Rodgers had tried anything like that on me, I would have made him knock it off and damned quick. We got to the sixth tee and Palmer was a tight bundle of nerves when he addressed his ball. His backswing looked very stiff. Tension was never going to win us anything, so I tried to settle him down. "All right, partner," I said, "this is a new hole. Nice smooth backswing and just lay it out there."

He stopped and turned on me! He, honest to God, turned on me, and said, "I'll keep it smooth if you'll keep it quiet."

Well, stupid me or something. I thought we were supposed to be partners or something. I mean, how do you like that? Here Rodgers is the one who is needling him and Palmer turns on me. I suppose he thinks he's got to live with people like Rodgers on the tour all year, but if he openly insults a member of the Greens Committee of the Fairwood Golf and Tennis Club, that's all right.

Listen. . . don't talk to me about professionals in sport. The minute you let a professional in, you can just let manners and traditions go right out the back door. Remember that celebrity-bridge tournament last year when Charles Goren was insulting to my wife? I mean it. I mean he was actually insulting. Well, don't let me get started on that.

Anyway. . . I am perfectly willing to admit that Palmer can hit the long ball. But, like so many of these pros, he doesn't use his brain. He doesn't try to think his way through a course. He tries to overpower it. And you know as well as I do that Fairwood does not give in to the bully.

The tees are set back on the ninth today. . . . If it comes to that, the tees are back on all the holes today. That isn't golf. That takes the finesse out of the game and makes it into some sort of weight-lifting contest. Anyway, with the tees set back, that turns the ninth into a very tight 340 yards indeed. But instead of playing it smart and cosying an iron over to the left, Palmer hit one of those long drives as if he was on television or something. It went about 285 yards, but instead of leaving the green open, he put me right in front of the trap. I tell you, the man has no sense of strategy. He's just a slammer who thinks he can bring Fairwood to its knees with his press clippings. Well, it takes something a bit more than that, let me tell you. Anyway, I decided that if we were ever going to win anything today, I was just going to have to be bold. So I took a wedge and laid a sweetheart of a shot up on the green for a sure birdie. But then Palmer blew this 35-footer and I had to try to scramble to get down in par. You probably saw how tricky the grass is around the north side of the cup today. It left me with the toughest two-footer on the course. I put the brakes on it, but the ball just skidded by. It was about all anyone could do from there. I could see Palmer giving a big exaggerated exhale as he sort of backhanded the ball into the cup. Well, I have got to admit it. I gave him a very sharp look. I told him right out it may be all right for him to take a day off and horse around, but I try to be serious about my golf.

He stopped and turned on me! He, honest to God, turned on me, and said, "I'll keep it smooth if you'll keep it quiet."

These professionals are so sensitive. Just because Palmer was off his game and fozzling it all around, he decided he'd had enough and just plain forget about anybody else. Anyway, he mumbled something about having a stomachache or being sick to his stomach or something and said he felt he was going to get a lot sicker if he kept on playing.

And with that he left the course. Listen! Don't tell me. I know these professionals. They will do anything to keep from having to own up to a bad round. He was sick of his score and sick of his game. . . that's what he was sick of and I can't say I blame him for that.

No. . . I have been a member here ever since Grandfather lent the club the property to build the course, but if Arnold Palmer is ever allowed back here again, you will have to do without me. Maybe I am just old-fashioned, but I think it is time these professionals remembered that golf is still supposed to be a game for gentlemen.

PLAYBOY'S PARTY JOKES

*T*WO MEN were playing golf and one of them was just setting up a putt on the third green when a nude girl rushed out of the trees nearby. She was being pursued by several distinguished-looking men in white coats. This didn't distract the dedicated golfers and they continued their game, only to see the same sight on the next two greens. Finally, they caught the attention of one of the men in white and asked him what was going on. "She's our patient," he explained, "and she has an obsession about running nude across a golf course."

"I see," said one of the golfers. "But why is your colleague carrying a bucket full of sand?"

"That's his handicap," replied the attendant. "He caught her yesterday."

"Listen, let's put away these silly clubs, run up to my place
and then you can really show me how to swing!"

"He claims it helps him to concentrate."

I'M NOT SURE G*O*L*F IS THERAPY

fiction By RICHARD HOOKER

hawkeye the sawbones, honorably discharged from m*a*s*h, discovers a civilian medic's lot is not a restful one

AS USUAL, my golf weekend began Friday night with a phone call from my partner Mr. Rat Regan, the history teacher at Lincoln Academy in Newcastle, Maine, who said, "Hey, Hawkeye, be strong tomorrow. We gotta clock those mothers.

"OK, Rat, I'll do my best."

ILLUSTRATION BY GILBERT STONE

"And try for the hat trick," Rat urged.

Hawkeye's hat trick assures a score of not over 76. It depends, first, on my ability to complete hospital rounds and get home not later than 10:40 A.M. Then, if my wife is in a happy, receptive mood, if the kids are farmed out and the tide is high, the hat trick has a chance. It is this: (1) Make love to wife at 10:50, (2) mix large gin and tonic at 11:05 and (3) take swim at 11:10.

Hawkeye's hat trick assures a score of not over 76. It is this: (1) Make love to wife at 10:50, (2) mix large gin and tonic at 11:05 and (3) take swim at 11:10.

In a good year, the hat trick may happen twice. August eighth was typical of 1970, which was not a good year at all, but the day started auspiciously. When I arose at six A.M., the sun shone and a glance at the cove indicated that the tide was just starting to come in. Finest swimming at 11:10. Downstairs, a peek in the booze closet revealed a new jug of Beefeater. At 6:10, Mary sleepily entered the kitchen. "Rat says I gotta be strong," I told her. "How about the hat trick? If I win today, I'll take you out to dinner."

"The kids are all going to your parents' and I'd like to go out to dinner."

With visions of hat trick and shooting maybe even 73, I drove 50 miles to the hospital, arriving at 7:15. I wanted to make rounds in an hour and be out before anybody showed up to bug me. First I went to the intensive-care unit, where Al Morton, who'd lost his lower esophagus and upper stomach four days earlier, wasn't breathing too well.

"Get a chest X ray," I ordered and went to other patients. At eight o'clock, having seen the other patients, I went to radiology for a look at Al's X ray, which showed fluid in his right chest.

Back in intensive care, I asked for a thoracentesis set. I put a needle in Al's chest and withdrew a syringeful of thin bloody fluid. Probably, I'd gotten into his right pleural cavity at surgery. "OK," I said, "gimme the vacuum bottles and let's suck this out."

The nurse gave me the proper bottle and looked happy with her efficiency. "Where's the rigamajig I stick into Al and hook into this bottle?" I asked.

"What?"

"Oh, Lord, it really *is* Saturday. You mean to tell me—oh, never mind. Just somebody find the tubing I need. It's supposed to come with the set."

Four nurses disappeared in four different directions—just like the day the cake of Ivory sank at Proctor & Gamble's. Visions of hat trick blurred. Al Morton sat on the edge of his bed, his arms resting on the bedside stand. "What the hell's wrong, Doc?" he asked.

Al's right pleural cavity was sucked dry and his breathing improved. I raced for the back door . . .

"All that's wrong, Al," I reassured him, "is that you got a quart of bloody juice in your right chest and nobody will provide me with the simple utensils to remove it. If you find this disturbing, think of me. You're hung here anyhow, but I got a shot at the hat trick and eighteen holes of golf."

Finally, a reluctant genie in central supply produced the proper tubing. Al's right pleural cavity was sucked dry and his breathing improved. I raced for the back door, flicked out the light opposite my name, stepped into the parking lot, visions of the hat trick clearly in focus, and heard the noise box say, "Dr. Hawkeye, emergency room." For a moment I kept going, but changed my mind. If it were important, I'd just have to come back. Better face up to it now.

In the emergency room, Dr. Doggy Moore, the general practitioner who sends me cases, said, "Hey, Hawk, you wanta take out an appendix?"

"No."

"Could you make a living without me?"

"No way."

"Then get ready. Examine the kid and change your clothes. I've already scheduled him. He has it."

By 9:30, the diseased appendix was out and the parents made happy. "I suppose you're in a hurry to get to the course," said Doggy. "I got two gall bladders in. You wanta see them now or Monday?"

"Monday."

"OK, I guess. One of them said she'd just as soon have someone else."

"I'll say hello to them. You got them all worked up? If so, I'll do one Monday and one Tuesday."

PLAYBOY'S PARTY JOKES

SAINT PETER challenged God to a heavenly golf match and, after Peter hit his tee shot close to the pin and God sliced badly into the rough, the twosome started hiking down the fairway. Suddenly a squirrel picked up the Lord's golf ball and darted away, only to be grasped by a huge eagle, which carried the little animal high into the sky. Dark clouds then filled the air as a thunderbolt struck the bird, causing it to release the squirrel, which, in turn, dropped the ball onto the green, where it bounced several times and rolled into the cup. "Damn it!" cried the exasperated saint. "Are you going to screw around or play golf?"

• • •

A YOUNG AMERICAN businessman visiting Tokyo knew no Japanese, but he nevertheless managed to persuade an attractive girl who spoke no English to accompany him to his hotel room. He felt proud of his prowess as the girl kept exclaiming, "Nachigai ana!" with considerable feeling during the sex act.

The following afternoon, he played golf with a prominent Japanese industrialist. When the latter happened to score a hole in one, the American decided to make some intercultural brownie points by shouting, "Nachigai ana!! Nachigai ana!" at the top of his voice.

The industrialist moved slowly and fixed him with a penetrating stare. "What you mean—the wrong hole?"

"If you'd let me join the damned country club, I'd
probably be out there playin' golf now. . . ."

"That's a good boy," said Doggy.

I finally left the hospital at 9:50, drove like hell, got home at 10:40 and found Mary mowing the lawn. "You'd think," she said, "that with five children and a husband, I wouldn't have to mow this great big lawn all by myself."

"You going to just complain all the time or do you want to go out to dinner tonight?"

"All I know is you better shoot seventy-six today or it'll be the last hat trick you ever get," she said lovingly as she slipped out of her shorts a few minutes later in our bedroom.

The phone rang. "Hawk, this is Clarence. I never figured to catch you home. I got a guy with a pneumothorax in Damariscotta. I think maybe you oughta see him. He's breathing hard."

Damariscotta is on my way to the golf course. Just time to cure pneumothorax and make tee-off time. "Sorry, honey," I said. "No hat trick. Gotta go. See you."

"How about dinner?"

"Sure, I even pay off on good intentions."

Arriving rapidly in Damariscotta, I put a Foley catheter in the patient's third anterior interspace and passed the time of day with Clarence while the lung expanded. At 11:55, I began the final leg of my journey to the Wawenock Country Club, where Dry Hole Pomerleau, the French well driller, inquired, "Where you been, you quack? You think we're going to keep on waiting for you, year in and year out?"

"Shut up and order me a cheeseburger while I get out my clubs."

"How many you knock off this week?" he persisted.

"None, unless you count Frenchmen. I want lunch. I don't want to listen to you."

Moments later, Dry Hole and I joined Rat Regan and Roy Jenkins, the 76-year-old hustler, for lunch in the combination sandwich and pro shop. "I see you're drivin' Benny's Cadillac today," observed Mr. Jenkins.

A year earlier, I'd operated on Benny for carcinoma of the pancreas. Benny lasted just long enough to make a will that bequeathed, to me, his new Cadillac. He did this with charity in his mind but also, I suspect, with malice in his heart. The word at Wawenock is: Don't buy a new car just before you get operated on by Hawkeye. Mr. Jenkins, every Saturday, mentions Benny's Cadillac just before saying, "Doc, you gotta start me two up."

Roy Jenkins—tall, lean, still strong—was Maine Open Champion in 1938 and I couldn't beat him with a rifle, but I always have to listen

"That's _pressure!_"

to his pitch, which, this day, was, "Gawd, Doc, I went fishin' last night. Got a hook caught in my finger. I shouldn't even be out here. Can't grab aholt of a club."

"Get to be ninety and cut off a hand, you old thief," I goad him, "and maybe I'll start you one up."

"I just don't know. When I was a young feller, I never talked to old folks like that."

The phone rang in the pro shop. "It's for you, Hawk," said the kid in charge.

"Hey, Hawkeye," said a happy, professional voice. "Glad I caught you. This is Joe Davis in Skowhegan. I want to talk to you about a guy who got shot in the chest."

"Talk to me, Joe."

"Well, I don't know. He's OK now, but he's got a lot of blood in there."

"You call it, Joe. I'll lay it on the line. I'd like to play golf and then come see him, but if you say come now, I will."

In the background, Jenkins was saying, "Listen to that. Somebody's sick, but that feller there wants to get out of it and play golf."

"Well, I don't know," said Joe.

"Tell you what, Joe. Tap his chest, see how he does, and if you get worried, call here and say it's an emergency. Someone will get me."

On the first tee, Rat Regan said, "You gotta be strong. You made the hat trick, didn't you? I called Mary at ten and she said it looked good."

"Just hit the ball, Rat. *You* better be strong."

"I just don't think it's fair, Doc," insisted Jenkins. "A big, strong young feller like you and I'm livin' on a fixed retirement income and you want to play me even."

"One more word and I'll operate on you with my driver."

"It could be worse, Roy," offered Dry Hole. "He could use a scalpel."

The first green at Wawenock is 349 yards from an elevated tee. A drive and a wedge. Stiff from riding, neither soothed nor relaxed by so much as one leg of the hat trick, I swing awkwardly, nearly fanning the ball, which went downhill about 100 yards.

"OK, Hawkeye, baby," said Rat, "not far, but you rammed it right down the middle."

For my second shot, I used a three wood and created a screaming duck hook that caromed off a rock to the left and 30 yards short of the green, bounced through a sand trap and came to rest eight feet from the pin. Dry Hole Pomerleau and Jenkins ignored me completely, but my partner, Rat, offered hearty congratulations. Just before putting, I looked back toward the clubhouse and saw a kid in a golf cart riding down the fairway. This always means a phone call for me and does not help my concentration. I stabbed the putt two feet short and way off line.

"The delicate hands of a surgeon," commented Dry Hole to Jenkins. "How'd you like to get operated on by *him*?"

"Hey, Hawk, emergency in Skowhegan," said the kid in the golf cart. He took me back to the clubhouse, where Joe Davis asked if he could send the patient to my hospital. I agreed, called there to leave orders and rode back to join my group on the second tee. Waiting for me, they'd had to allow another foursome, including Dud Clement, the undertaker, to go through.

"Well, well," said the prominent funeral director, "if it isn't the Doctor of the Year. I'm hoping for a quiet weekend. You haven't operated on anyone from this area recently, have you?"

"Hit the ball and shut up," I growled.

"We're having our annual convention at the Samoset next week," said Dud. "You're up for re-election. Just think of it. You got a chance of being Doctor of the Year twice in a row!"

"Hey, Dud," asked old man Jenkins, "is it true you and Hawkeye is splittin' fees?"

Finally, even without the hat trick, I got it going. After hitting a trap on three and taking a double bogey, I birdied four and was only two over after eight holes when the golf cart came again. No way out this time. I drove 50 miles back to the hospital, where the patient with the gunshot chest was, it turned out, in no real trouble, but I had to be sure.

Arriving home at 5:30, I poured out my woes. "Oh, my poor dear, you've had a hard day, haven't you?" Mary said as she sat on my lap and kissed me. "Tell you what—the tide's too low for swimming, but you could still have two-thirds of a hat trick."

"Get away from me, you sex-crazy maniac," I ordered, pushing her out of my lap. "Just bring me a great big gin and tonic."

"*Joe, I hate to mention this when we have a double press going, but do you and Mary have a house guest?*"

"I asked what she was doing out here, and she says she's
looking for a ball, too."

PLAYBOY'S PARTY JOKES

*T*HE TWO EXECUTIVES had never golfed together before and the first man up took out a new ball, placed it on the tee and proceeded to slice it into the woods to the right of the fairway. Unable to find it in the thick underbrush, he put another new ball on the edge of the fairway and this time he drove it over a fence. Putting a third new ball in position, he then proceeded to hit it into the middle of the lake.

As he was preparing to shoot yet another new golf ball from the edge of the lake, the second executive said to their caddy, "I don't understand why a guy who loses so many continues to shoot a brand-new ball every time."

The caddy shook his head, saying, "Maybe he's never had any used ones."

• • •

*T*HE MINISTER who had just joined the golf club turned up at the first tee looking like any other Saturday-morning player in his sport shirt and slacks. He had difficulty in finding a partner, though, until he was finally approached by a man who suggested that they play a round together for two dollars a hole. The clergyman agreed but soon regretted his decision as he began to lose every hole. Upon seeing the minister change back into clerical garb at the end of the game, the man muttered apologetically, "I'm sorry, Reverend, but I wouldn't have taken your money if I had known you were a preacher. You see, I'm the club pro."

"That's quite all right," said the minister benignly. "To prove there are no hard feelings, you bring your parents around sometime and I'll be glad to marry them."

"C'mon, admit it, Francesca—you're not even
interested in how I broke ninety!"

the high-class hustle

article

by william barry furlong

*an expert's guide
to the changing face
of golf-course larceny*

THE AIR had a fabricated chill, the slight odor of chemistry and compressors. In a couple of hours, the bar's night lights would come on, enhancing every wrinkle, mole, pimple with the merciless cruelty of motel-bathroom lighting. "You can't make money sitting in a place like this," said the Archivist irritably. He was talking of the way he makes money—by hustling golf—not the way the barkeep does it. He was a short man, in his mid-to-late 30s, beginning to lean to fat. There was about him the very faint but perceptible flavor of kinetic violence, an attribute for a man who—having to "collect"—always seems on the edge of losing his temper. Even when motionless, he exudes a quality of beefy energy or dramatic command. His skull is large under the wavy, dark

SCULPTURE BY PARVIZ SADIGHIAN

hair, his face is theatrical—with heavy bones and eyes that slant downward at the outside corners. A small mouth, expressive brows, a general look of gamy handsomeness that you might cast as the hard-drinking private eye of a low-budget television serial. He is single, a man oriented to good whiskey, good cigars, good women and cutthroat poker for high stakes. He is modest, falsely, about one thing—his golf swing ("a good enough swing for a short, fat little guy")—and embarrassed about another: He makes a legitimate living. Sometimes.

"The old days are gone. You've got to have something legitimate now. People know you're a hustler and they avoid you. Unless you're a big-time pro, a celebrity. Then they think it's a privilege to lose to you." So he sells insurance. To his astonishment, he sells a lot of it. It is easy to see why. He has, when he chooses, the ability to relate totally to someone, to listen to what he has to say with an intensity that makes him feel unique, to give that someone the feeling that he or she is the most perceptive person he's ever encountered. His is an exercise in the pragmatics of instant intimacy. ("I sell a lot of insurance to divorcées and widows," he says dryly. And even that is the least of the premium.) It is, of course, all counterfeit; he is also sly, devious and single-minded. "That's why I hustle golf," he says. "I'm a natural."

Golf, in fact, has always been a game that appealed to the single-minded, the simple-minded and the devious—the hustled as well as the hustler. Take single-mindedness: Ask a golfer about Dick Nixon and he'll say, "Used too much right hand." Or simple-mindedness: Ask a golfer what the essence of the game is and he'll say skill, because he hasn't realized the truth—self-deception. Or deviousness: Ask a golfer what the rules are and he'll say, "Something to break." Perhaps this is the reason that golf is so popular: Men can get a lot of sun and fun while succumbing triumphantly to their lower instincts. For no other obsession this side of the White House offers so superb an opportunity for chicanery, duplicity and all-round villainy as does golf. The reason is not only the existence of rules but their abundance; they range in style, tone and amplitude from the polished-mahogany politeness of the Royal and Ancient in Scotland to the spontaneous perfidies of Goat Hill in East Wagering. They are, in their opportunity, what appeals to most men: Any individual lacking in power, youth, speed, brawn, clearness of eye, suppleness of muscle, virtue of purpose can become a pretty good golfer. And hustler.

"As long as he has style," says the Archivist. He earned the cognomen because (a) no hustler wants to be known—if he's known at all—by his real name and (b) because it fits: He not only hustles but he memorializes hustling by becoming something of a storehouse for the rich, arcane legends and traditions of the felony. He has studied the techniques of hustling, amateur and otherwise, from his own high-style hustle back to the raffish days of the talented tramp—the days of the Stork, the Fat Man, the Dog Man, the Fire Man, Mysterious Montague, Titanic Thompson, and so on and on. He considers himself and his style an aberration—or an accommodation—of the times. He has never made the "hustlers' rounds"— Edgewater and Tam O'Shanter and Riverwoods in and around Chicago, Tension Park in Dallas, Memorial Park in Houston, Bayshore in Miami. "Most of those places are reformed or sold for developments," he says. This is not to say he doesn't make the Miami Beach rounds. "I spend six/eight weeks down there every winter." Not always consecutively: He'll work the rounds according to his pigeon's vacation cycle, then fly back to Chicago for some midweek insurance selling ("I got to keep the business going—just at that rate, so it doesn't come to possess me") before flying back for a new cycle of vacationers—and victims. He spends the summer the same way, playing very little midweek golf in the Chicago area— "You heard of never dirtying your own nest?"—before flying off for long weekends of golf in the Catskills or in Texas or anyplace where men care not whether they win or lose but how much they play the game for. He likes to consider himself a golfer, not a gambler. ("The hustlers in the past were all gamblers; they got famous as gamblers because they couldn't hack it as golfers.") And he insists that it is not the hustle he's interested in but the psychology of the hustle. "People *need* to be hustled. They've got to take the grand chance— the big bet that they're going to lose. They put themselves in the way of it: You lose at golf, you feel you've made the big bid, but what have you lost? Your life? Nothing! You lost some money—which you substitute for your life!" He translates this into a readiness to be psyched out—"Even the biggest of the big-time golfers get psyched out and they do it because they need to."

One of his earliest memories of golf was the 1947 U.S. Open— "I was ten, eleven years old"—in St. Louis, when Sam Snead met Lew Worsham in a play-off. They were on the 18th green of the play-off, still tied and with the balls almost identical distances from the hole. Snead was about to putt, because he believed he was "away," when Worsham stepped in front of him and asked, "What are you doing?"

"I'm putting out," said Snead.

"Oh, no," said Worsham. "I think I'm away and should have the first putt." He called for a tape measure. In the meantime, Snead had to step back and, in utter fury, wait for the putting distances to be measured. It turned out that Worsham's ball was 30 inches from the cup and Snead's ball was 30 and a half inches away. So Snead *did* have the right to putt first. But he'd been psyched out. When he got up to the ball, his concentration was broken and he blew the putt by two inches. Worsham, barely controlling the grin, stepped up, hit his putt smack into the cup and won the play-off and the U.S. Open.

"It was the closest Snead ever came to winning an Open and he was beaten on a psych-out trick," says the Archivist. "The thing about Snead is that *not* winning the Open is his thing. He's more famous for not winning than he is for winning. He was psyched out on that hole, but maybe he *had* to be psyched out. The way I look at it, there are times when even a Snead has to be a loser."

> *"He was psyched out on that hole, but maybe he had to be psyched out. The way I look at it, there are times when even a Snead has to be a loser."*

So he began studying not only the hustling of golf but the psychology of the hustle. He got to caddying at Tam O'Shanter, "a great place for studying. A legitimate golf club—everything on the up-and-up, but a place where people went to find action." He found the psych-out as cordial as a bloodletting among friends. He tends to classify the "friendly" psych-outs in this way:

The admiring cut: You admire your opponent in just the right way for an extravagantly bad shot. "Not bad, not bad at all. There's the ball over there, under the rock next to the tree. Another two or three shots like that and you'll be off the tee."

The helpful cut: You wait until the opponent is in his backswing and then say helpfully, "Don't worry too much about the water on the right." Or you comment, "Say, do you always hold your right hand over like that?" A more elegant example of the form was—says the Archivist—displayed by comedian Buddy Hackett, a golfer more enthusiastic than skilled. Hackett, he says, goes onto the course with a package of Band-Aids and, when somebody is doing something disgustingly well, he offers one to him.

"Here, you'll need this for your finger," he says.

"What finger? What are you talking about?" says the opponent.

"Just to take care of those blisters in that one spot. . . from the funny way you hold the club."

"Wha'd'ya mean, the funny way I hold the club?"

"Oh, nothin'. Don't give it a second thought. Just keep the Band-Aids handy. When the blisters pop, you'll be glad you have them."

That, says the Archivist, "should be good for three strokes a round."

The distractive cut: You wait until your opponent is standing over a key shot and then you say, "Oh, I forgot to tell you. Met your doctor in the clubhouse and he wants to talk to you as soon as our round is over about the X rays you had last week. Nothing to worry about—just something about that dark spot on your lungs."

Or, if your opponent happened to be out of town for a few days and elects to go right from the airport to the first tee—as any thoughtful man would—it's helpful to pick up his wife and drive her over to the golf course for the joyful reunion. The uniform is an unshaven face and clothes that look like you've slept in them. Then, as you leave her and approach the first tee, you turn and wave to her and say warmly, "I'll never forget." When her husband/your opponent hears someone looking like *you're* looking say "I'll never forget" to his wife, you can be sure *he* won't forget, either.

The curious cut: You ask an innocent question about his game—the best part of his game—so that he begins to dissect what he's doing well reflexively. "Did you realize that you tap your right foot three times every time you putt?" is a good question. ("It took me five years to get my putting back to form—I was looking at my foot all the time instead of the putt," one victim has said.) Of course, sometimes the ploy doesn't work.

On the eve of the British Amateur at Sandwich in 1948, says the Archivist, a British golf writer sent a note to a fellow diner, Frank Stranahan, asking: "Do you inhale or exhale when putting?" The idea, of course, was to get Stranahan, a most accomplished golfer, to think about his breathing, not his putting.

At the adjoining table, Stranahan looked up, apparently bewildered. "I don't know," he said.

Later that evening, the writer noticed—with satisfaction—Stranahan on the practice green, inhaling on one shot, exhaling on the next. He must have found the answer, because the last laugh was on the Britisher. Inhaling and exhaling all the way, Stranahan won

*"Look! There goes one of the touring pros
with one of the touring pros."*

the tournament, beating the local favorite, Charles Stowe of Sandwich, five and four.

The Archivist spent his caddying years studying not only the psychology of hustling but some of its tactics and personalities. "All the hustlers then had a 'freak-shot bet.' If they lost to you in a game of golf, they'd come right back at you with their freak bet that you figured you couldn't lose. The Stork would bet you he could win—on a handicap—by standing on one foot for every shot; he'd tuck one leg up behind him. Mysterious Montague would bet you he could beat you on the putting green with a rake, a hoe or a shovel." Charley the Blade would bet he could beat you playing only with a three iron. Floren DiPaglia, who went from fixing basketball games to hustling golf—a natural progression—used to bet high-handicap golfers that he could beat them even though he played all his tee shots with a Dixie Cup over the ball. George Low, once a pro-tour golfer, would bet you he could win putting by *kicking* the ball into the hole ("He's supposed to have aced five of nine holes that way on one bet") and—if it meant a great hustling opportunity—he'd bet you he could win on the greens using a rake, a broom handle or a pool cue. Lee Trevino, who hustled bets on a par-three course in Dallas before going on the pro tour, would bet he could beat you using a taped-up Dr. Pepper bottle ("He wasn't so dumb; it had a smooth side instead of the bulging ribs that Coke bottles have"). And Snead has been known to hack a club out of a branch from a swamp-maple tree and bet a "mullet" (as he called his victims) he could beat him using the stick for tee and fairway shots and a wedge for chipping and putting. The mullet took the bet eagerly—and paid off when Snead shot a 76.

In the old days, says the Archivist, the most florid and renowned hustler was a tall, lean itinerant named Titanic Thompson. "He was a gambler as much as a golfer," says the Archivist, "so he wasn't always working the hustle in expected ways." Once he made a bet with some pigeon that he could drive a ball 500 yards off the tee of his choice. Since the world record recognized by the Professional Golfers Association is 392 yards and the longest known drive was that of a 483-yard hole in Devon, England, with a gale to help, Titanic's bet seemed like a good one to the pigeon. Only the tee Titanic chose, outside Chicago, had a steep drop-off far down the fairway and—while the fairway dog-legged right—the course ran straight out to Lake Michigan. As it happened, Titanic chose winter to carry out the bet, so not only was the fairway ice-hard but so was the water of the lake. The ball had only to take a couple of big bounces before it was heading out over the ice in the general direction of Michigan. It went not only 500 yards but perhaps that many miles.

If he lost a bet, somehow Titanic had a way to get even: He'd pull out a gun and bet double or nothing he could split a silver dollar thrown into the air—he was, among other things, an expert shot. Or he'd bet he could throw a quarter into a skinned potato at 15 feet—for some reason, he was an expert at that, too. If it had been a really bad day, he'd have some back-to-the-clubhouse bets. One example: On the course he'd usually be tossing pecans into the air and catching them in his mouth. When he got back to the clubhouse, he'd bet everybody double or nothing that he could toss one of the nuts over the clubhouse roof to the other side. Whereupon, he'd palm the selected pecan, replace it with a lead-filled pecan and throw *it* over the clubhouse. If anybody objected, he'd say, "I threw a pecan like we bet. Nobody said what it had to be filled with." But this gimmick became fairly well known and when its allure wore off, he'd bet he could throw a pumpkin over the roof. The pumpkin happened to be one he'd reserved for the purpose—it was the size of a baseball—and he'd win the bet easily.

If he lost a bet, somehow Titanic had a way to get even: He'd pull out a gun and bet double or nothing he could split a silver dollar thrown into the air—he was, among other things, an expert shot.

Some bets demanded more in the way of resourcefulness. One day Titanic was on the putting green at Tenison Park, practicing with a long-handled shovel—on the chance someone might want to bet that he could beat Titanic putting with a shovel—when a wealthy used-car dealer approached with a deal he couldn't refuse.

"See that kid over there?" he asked. Titanic saw a long-haired kid putting with a wedge and picking the ball out of the hole with his toes. "I'll back him against you for a grand," said the used-car dealer.

There is nothing that arouses a hustler so much as a chance to match mind and morals with a used-car dealer—particularly one

PLAYBOY'S PARTY JOKES

*I*N AN EFFORT to become closer with her golf-playing boyfriend, a young woman hired a club pro for instruction. The first morning, he took her out to the eighteenth green to help her get a feel for the game. The novice watched as a golfer struggled to get out of a bunker. After several whiffs, the ball finally rose in a cloud of sand, dropped on the green and rolled into the hole.

"Oh, boy," she sighed. "He'll have one hell of a time getting out of that one."

exploiting a kid who can't even afford to buy shoes. It never even dawned on Titanic that the kid—like himself—may not have been altogether what he seemed.

He was, in fact, one of the best junior players in the state. He could outhit Titanic—who was in his upper years—off the tee with no trouble. It was only slightly more trouble to demolish him entirely over the 18 holes.

While the kid went back to the first tee to take on the next pigeon, Titanic went off to brood for a while. He moped around the clubhouse, pitching coins at a crack in the floor—another hobby of his—until he could catch the used-car dealer with a deal *he* couldn't refuse. "I'll play him double or nothing and I'll beat him," he said. "And to show you how confident I am, I'll let him take *three* drives off each tee and then let him play his best one." The patron leaped at the chance; some used-car dealers have absolutely no morals about how and how much they exploit a pigeon.

In the first nine holes, the kid began piling up a good lead. It wasn't always easy: This was the third round the kid was playing on this day and—with the extra strokes off each tee—it was the equivalent of two or three extra rounds in one. By the 11th hole, the kid's arms began showing some of the wear of trying to make three long drives off each tee. He began hooking the ball viciously in strenuous efforts to maintain his distance, and then when he shifted his hands in the grip to compensate for it, he began fading it. Soon he couldn't get any of his three drives onto the fairway and by the 15th or 16th hole, when he overreacted in an effort to stay accurate, he wound up shooting short. Titanic finished the round by humiliating the kid and maintaining the honor of the hustler over the used-car dealer.

Titanic is in his 80s now. He kept hustling when he could no longer play well with yet another ploy. He tutored a group of kid golfers in how to make certain shots, then he'd send them out to play the game after he used *his* head to arrange the hustle. ("Maybe I can't beat you, but my caddy can.") In a sense, says the Archivist, the passing of Titanic signaled the passing of old-time hustling. "Not much action in the old sense around nowadays. It's all penny-ante stuff." He feels the old-time hustlers brought it on themselves: "You got to want to be a freak, a carny, to wander around the country looking for suckers who bet they can beat you when you're standing on one foot with a heel on your ass." People got to know you because you *were* a freak and you had to move on—one day here, the next day 500 miles down the road, the day after that 500 miles farther down the road. "That's the penny-ante life." He much prefers the high-class hustle among "high-class people who are a success in life and are out on the golf course looking to be losers." Not only at golf: "Hell, they have their bookmakers following them around the course for the afternoon's action at Hialeah, they stop at every phone to call their brokers to see how they're doing in the market." The difference for him is not only in the suckers but in a style of life. "I've got my roots down and I've got a business. The insurance gives me a parlay on the golf—I get a little business on the course, I get a little golf in through the business." Most of all, it gives him an acceptable identity—i.e., anything but as a hustler. "In the old days, all the hustlers didn't mind being known as hustlers. They just didn't want to be known as themselves." Even Titanic kept his real name—Alvin C. Thomas—a secret. Not anymore. "People know you're a hustler and they stay away from you." So the hustler today wants an identity not as a hustler or even a golfer. "Diz Dean has an identity—he hustles all the time and people don't mind losing to him, because they think of him as a *baseball* player." He mentions another baseball player, now a coach, who labors hard at *not* being known as a golfer. "Hell, he was about to break the course record one day and—so word wouldn't get around about how good a golfer he was—he double-bogeyed the last two holes." The Archivist keeps a very low profile campaigning as a businessman, as an exceptionally winning insurance agent. In doing so, he adheres to a fundamental proposition: He doesn't cheat his victims—he just places them in the way of cheating themselves. "I mean, hell, they're *dying* to do it."

He identifies three areas in which the system works in the high-class hustle:

Always know how to lose a little on the exotic bets so you can win a lot in the end.

Always give the guy who's gross in trying to cheat himself a reasonable opportunity to do it.

Always know so much about your game and his that you can make honest and reasonable bets that it's very unlikely you'll lose.

As an example of the first principle, he cites the bet known as bingle-bangle-bungle, a not uncommon bet in hustling, or in the friendly little bloodletting of weekends in the open air. It's basically a three-way bet on a particular hole—usually a par four.

Bingle is a bet on who'll hit the first ball to land on the green. Its payoff is a minimum figure—say $50.

Bangle is a bet on who has the ball that's closest to the cup after all the balls are on the green. Its payoff is for a middling figure—say $100.

Bungle—or bunko to some—is a bet on who gets the ball into

"Why don't you drop another ball? I think you looked <u>everywhere</u>!"

the cup first. It's for the third and highest payoff—say $150.

Each bettor in a foursome puts up $75 on the bet; each member of a threesome has to put up $100.

"The thing about this bet is that any golfer—even a high-handicap golfer—can win it," says the Archivist. "But he's so anxious to win it all that he cheats himself out of the big-money end of it."

How?

"By not having the good sense to lose the front end of the bet purposefully." The front end is designed to lure the pigeon: "It's the classic play in golf—who gets onto the green first is really another way of saying who makes it in the least number of strokes. Who can

> *"The thing about this bet is that any golfer—even a high-handicap golfer—can win it," says the Archivist. "But he's so anxious to win it all that he cheats himself out of the big-money end of it."*

get up there and power the ball the farthest? So it's a familiar bet—the pigeon reacts reflexively to it. But the guy who gets onto the green first has practically no chance of winning the second and third legs of the bet. He's going to be too far away to win the second leg or the third leg." And there's one more point: He's going to be swinging so hard to get his drive out there that he may wind up in the rough or the woods or the water or a sand trap. "So he's going to try to win the low end of the bet—hell, $50 won't give him his investment back—and he stands a good chance to lose it all."

What the hustler does is lose the first bet. Deliberately. "I play what looks like hacker's golf—worse than the worst," he says. "I look for the best lie off the tee—I don't care how short it is. I want to find my way up there so on my final approach shot I can pitch right up to the cup." It doesn't bother him if it takes him three, four or five strokes to get to the green, as long as he's closest to the cup when he gets there. "This second bet pays off on distance, not on least strokes—this is what the pigeons don't understand. Once I give up the least-strokes idea—once I give up the $50 bet—I get in a position to win the $100. With $150 to come on bungle, because I am *closest* to the hole, I got the best putt of them all."

The third phase of the bet relies, for the hustler, on his verbal skill as much as his golfing skill. For if he's been swift and foresighted on the tee, he'll have arranged that all putting will be done in strict rotation, instead of in the normal course of the "most away" man getting the first putt, the "next most away" getting the second putt, and so on. "If we use the regular rules, I'll always putt last," says the Archivist. "That means anybody else can get lucky and sink a long putt and beat me. But if we putt by rotation, I may be the guy who comes up first in the rotation. Or second. Or third. Anyway, I come off better. No way can I come off worse."

Even if he happens to putt third or fourth, he figures to have an advantage. "The other guys—who were so fast after the first fifty bucks—will see what I've done and they'll be so mad at having been foxed that they can't concentrate on their putts. I'll even tell them about it, if they're so dumb they've missed the point." He'll needle, he'll brag, he'll infuriate—he'll get them to the point where he figures that they'll be so mad they'll blow their putts. His point is that then he's got them two ways: on distance and on concentration. "I haven't done anything but play the first shot the way the worst possible golfer would play it—short and safe. And then I tell them about it."

To illustrate the second principle—"You see a guy who's a sneak and you let him think he's sneaking an advantage"—the Archivist cites the art of the Fat Man. His name was Martin Stanovich, an awkward, bulbous man who straddled the ball like a hacker—and then executed some of the most wondrous shots known to man. The Fat Man didn't mind playing an opponent who could outdrive him. In fact, he'd frequently fall short of the tee of an opponent who *couldn't* outdrive him. The reason was that he'd then have first shot on the fairway. Both he and his opponent would stop first at his ball and that gave the opponent a deceptive advantage: He could see what club the Fat Man would select from the spot on the fairway and—figuring that he himself was perhaps five or ten yards closer to the pin—choose his own club accordingly.

There was just one small thing: Stanovich covered the clubs with the wrong covers.

He'd turn to his caddy and say, "Give me the five iron." The caddy would reach for the iron covered with a 5, strip the cover and hand it to the Fat Man. It was really a seven iron and the Fat Man would pop the ball gently onto the green, three feet from the cup.

His opponent would walk up, measure the distance, turn to the caddy and say, "Give me the five iron." Only he'd really get the five iron. He'd swing and club the ball 30 yards over the green and spend three strokes trying to find his way back out of the woods.

The Fat Man would smile enigmatically. He'd done nothing wrong. He simply allowed his opponent the chance to cheat himself.

The reverse twist on this—"there's always a reverse twist"—is to let the opponent cheat himself on the fact that you *can* outdrive him. "This is the Dick Martin bit." Dick Martin, a frail, skittish little man who makes his living playing golf down in East Dallas, once played five guys with high handicaps in a best-ball round. That meant that he'd play his round and they could pick the best of their five lies on each shot to match against his. Thus, they could use the best of their five skills against his encapsulated skill. But he could outdrive all of them—a fact that he knew and they knew. And so, grudgingly, terribly reluctantly, he yielded one extra point: They could start play with their second shot—from where his tee shot landed. That figured to give them the best of all possible worlds: They'd have him drive for them and they could use the best man for each shot thereafter—the best man with the long iron, the best with the short iron, the best with the wedge, the best putter.

There was just one thing: On that day, Dick Martin suddenly developed a long and wicked hook. It was so bad and so devious that somehow the ball always landed in the worst of all possible spots—deep in the woods, in the shallows of a creek, on rock-strewn paths, in the next fairway. Martin had to play his way back from these disastrous shots, but he was always able to do it. His opponents also had to play their way back from these shots, but they weren't able to do it. The match was supposed to go nine holes. Martin won the first five and—since the pigeons could not possibly win—it was all over.

The third principle is simply to think about golf and the golf course in a way that lets the Archivist measure his game against his opponent's—with the golf course giving him the edge.

"The great golf courses, the great holes are really triumphs of psychology—they look like they're going to give you something while they take something away," he says. "It's a setup that's ideal for hustling."

Thus, he looks carefully at the course and its psychological play. He can glance at the layout, for example, and tell what kind of golfer its overall design might favor.

"Most of the courses built from around the turn of the century to about the mid-sixties favored a right-handed golfer with a hook,"

*"When we or if we ever get back to the clubhouse,
I think we should have a word with the
course planning committee."*

PLAYBOY'S PARTY JOKES

As a golfer teed up at precisely his reserved time, he was tapped on the shoulder. The intruder handed him a note reading, "I am deaf and mute. Please let me play through."

"This is my tee-off time," the golfer bellowed, shaking his head vigorously. "Your handicap doesn't entitle you to play through." Then he proceeded to drive his ball straight down the fairway.

"Nice shot," the fellow's caddy said as they headed off the tee, leaving the deaf-mute fuming.

While lining up his next shot, the golfer was struck on the head by a ball. Turning around angrily, he spotted the deaf-mute holding up his hand. "What the hell is he doing?" the golfer said, squinting into the sun.

"I believe he's holding up four fingers, sir," his caddy replied.

• • •

MacDermott and MacDuff were sitting in front of the clubhouse fireplace after 18 holes of golf on a raw, blustery day. The ice slowly melted from their beards and collected in puddles under their chairs. Outside, the wind continued to howl off the North Sea and hail beat against the windows.

The pair sat in silence over straight whiskies. Finally, MacDermott spoke. "Next Saturday, same time?"

"Aye," MacDuff replied gruffly, "weather permittin'."

🐰

he says. The reason is that most of them were built in or close to urban areas with busy roads around them. "The golfer in those days had played just enough to get rid of his slice and develop a hook. So they began building golf courses in a general counterclockwise fashion for the right-handed golfer with a hook." Why counterclock-

"If I've got a guy on a course like this who hits a high, lofty drive that hooks a little, I've got an edge on the bet that he hasn't even thought about."

wise? "Because if they built them clockwise, the right-handed hook would always be going off the golf course—physically off the golf course and onto the streets where there were people walking or driving. By building them counterclockwise, the right-handed hook still goes far off the fairway—maybe a couple of fairways over—but it still stays on the course: You don't endanger the people outside." (Needless to say, the golf course that favors the right-handed hook also favors the left-handed fade or slice.) "Not every course is built this way," he cautions. Firestone in Akron is built in a series of parallel holes and many of the most recent courses are so far away from highly trafficked streets that they can be built clockwise as readily as counterclockwise ("LaCosta out in California is an example").

Beyond that, the Archivist looks to the individual personality of the particular course he's playing—or lusting—on. "You take Colonial in Fort Worth. It's got Bermuda grass, which means the ball doesn't get much of a roll. You got a duffer who hits the ground shot and he won't get 120 yards there if he is used to getting 140—150 yards somewhere else. Also, it's a driver's course. If you've got a guy who can't hit hard and accurately off the tee, you know he's going to be in trouble on every hole." Also, it tends to favor the carefully controlled fade—"seven of the nine most difficult driving holes bend to the right." Its overall demand: "low, hard-punched shots—line drives, really—that don't get high enough to be caught by the wind. Normally, you get a lot of roll on that kind of shot after the ball hits the ground, and roll can get you into trouble, because once the ball hits the ground, it might hit anything on the ground and go anywhere. But with Bermuda, you're not going to get that roll. So you get the yardage without the danger." And, of course, the tee and fairway shots should be susceptible to a controlled fade. "If I've got a guy on a course like this who hits a high, lofty drive that hooks a little, I've got an edge on the bet that he hasn't even thought about."

Augusta National is just the opposite. "You need the high shot that you can drop down for a short roll pretty much where you want it. And a draw is a help here"—the most difficult holes bend to the left. "That's what Trevino meant when he said he didn't have the shots for the Masters. He's got a low punched drive that just can't do him as much good here as somewhere else. Give me Trevino against any golfer of equal skills who has a high, lofty shot with a short roll and I gotta take the other guy." That, he adds, is the reason Arnold Palmer changed his style of driving. "He hit the low, hard-punched shot—great for driving on those English and Scottish courses in the British Open—but he picked up the high, lofty shot with the short roll so that he would do better in the Masters."

The Archivist takes the same psychology down to a lower level: the individual hole. "There's a gate to the green—an opening—on every golf hole in the world," he says. "Most of them are quite obvious. You just go up the middle and find the gate to the green sitting fat out front—no sweat, no trouble." But the better golf courses will put the opening to the green off in a corner or at an oblique angle that will take the golfer out of his way if he wants to avoid hazards. "You can still get to the green if you want to go over water or over a sand trap," says the Archivist. "But if you want to get up there without encountering trouble, you're going to have to pay a price." The price, he says, is usually an extra stroke. "The easiest way in is the longest way around. You can take the easy way with more strokes or the hard way with fewer strokes. That's the test of golf—you give a little, you take a little." But that one extra stroke on every hole in a round—by a guy who's looking for the easy opening to the green— turns a 72-par into a 90. "Hell, I'm hustling for a stroke against a guy who doesn't know how the course is costing him 18 strokes."

And that's only the start, says the Archivist. "You analyze the good holes on the golf courses, and each one has a 'psychology'— they're trying to make you do something that's going to add to your score. How many guys you meet who know *that*? They're playin' the hole and they don't even know its psychology." He uses as an example the sixth hole at Seminole Golf Club near Palm Beach. ("Once, maybe twice a year I'm lucky enough to play it. That's the only time they let outsiders on the course—two members-guests tournaments

"Do my arms go over or under, Mr. Jackson?"

a winter." That's also why he's a "businessman," not a hustler.) The sixth is a 383-yard par-four hole—not a long one but a hole liberally sprinkled with trouble. "Constant sand. Like the Sahara. They got at least 11 sand traps in those 383 yards. You can't even see the fairway." The opening to the green is through a narrow channel of 150 yards down to the left of the fairway: on the right side of that channel are four huge sand traps. "But they give you that psychology right off the tee. You can *see* the opening to the left, but they block it out off the tee so that you feel you *have* to go to the right." The way it's done is by building bunkers a fewscore yards off the tee, invading from the left toward the right, as well as a few palm trees that force the curve of the fairway to the right. "Every psychological demand is made on the golfer to shoot to the right," says the Archivist. But this, of course, takes him away from the opening to the green. "So when the tee shot gets out there on the fairway, the golfer has two choices: One is to keep going down the right side and come across the big bunkers that guard the green on the right: the other is to sacrifice a shot on the fairway and try to cross over early to the left to get into the channel that leads to the green." The first way, the psychology of the hole leads the golfer into danger that might cost him several strokes. The second way, it leads him into the sacrifice of at least a stroke in the effort to "buy safety." "If he's strong psychologically, he'll take the risk—and lose bets. If not, he'll buy safety—and lose bets." What does the Archivist do? "I go over the bunkers off the tee and try to thread the opening between the palm trees on the left and the big bunker on the right. I'm closer to the hole and I've got no worse lie than if I was off to the right."

To accomplish all this—to respond to the psychology of the particular hole and golf course—the Archivist worked on perfecting all his golf shots. "The point of the high-class hustle is to be a good golfer, not just a good gambler," he says. So he can hit the fade as well as the draw, the low punched line drive as well as the soaring lofty fly ball that drops, bounces once or twice, and then stops with virtually no roll. He worked on getting out of all kinds of sand traps so hard that shooting out of a bunker poses no more psychological hazard to him than shooting out of a difficult fairway lie. The result is that he'd rather play a golf course with a lot of sand than one with a lot of water. "Water is impartial. It treats every golfer the same way. Once you get into it, you pay the same penalty for getting out as the worst duffer. But sand"—and his eyes light up with joy—"is a hustler's paradise. It treats me better than it treats most golfers simply because I worked hard to learn how to get out of it. It might cost me a stroke where it'll cost most other golfers two or three. That's where I get my insurance."

It is by measuring the course against the competition that he decides how to handle his bet. "On a well-bunkered course, I figure I'm going to have an edge on the other golfer that he won't even know about," he says. The basic bet is on the round, based on each golfer's handicap: The Nassau, for example, is a three-way bet—on who has fewest strokes on the first nine holes, who has fewest strokes on the second nine holes and who has fewest for the 18-hole total, with the handicap of each golfer figured into each score. "I won't lie about my golf game," he says about negotiating with his colleagues and victims. "I may test the truth a little, just to see how sharp they are, what their giving point is. But I'm not keeping any secrets from them. One round, two rounds, and you can't fool 'em anymore." What he can do is introduce a certain flexibility into the betting so that their handicaps may fit his skills in such a way as to give him an edge. "I *may* give a guy a half a stroke a hole except for the par threes," he says. That amounts to a seven-stroke giveaway, since there are usually four par threes on an 18-hole layout. "Or maybe I'll give him two strokes on the par fives and one stroke on the par fours, or maybe if he's a poor driver, I'll give him a stroke on every hole over 400 yards." That may not be as much of a concession as it seems, for he may know that the long holes demand a certain kind of driving ability—other than sheer distance—which the usual duffer does not have. "So that he's not only short but likely to be in trouble all the way," says the Archivist. If the trouble involves sand traps, not water, the Archivist figures he's got an edge of several strokes, simply because he knows he can "let out" and take the chance of the "sand-trap kind of trouble" on a long drive, "whereas the other guy is going to be short and have trouble anyway." If he's playing old friends—"guys I've been playing and betting with a long time"—he may let them have par for a partner on everything but, say, the par-five holes. That means the "friend" will always get the lower of two scores—either his score or par—on 14 holes. ("If he birdies it, he gets the birdie. If he bogeys it, he gets par.") But on the par five, he gets only the score he shoots. "That puts a lot more pressure on him—most golfers are psyched out by par-five holes, anyway. They're scared of them because the par fives are so long. This play just puts a little more pressure on them on the par five. Because when they see they're on some 'monster' hole and now they can't fall back on par, they're going to clutch—they're going to blow that hole skyhigh." And when they see how smoothly he plays the par fives—"If it's well bunkered, it's all to my advantage"—the pressure on them will rise even higher. "That's the psychology of the

"*There's nothing in the book that says I can't!*"

hustle: You give 'em a little one place, you take it away from 'em another place. They psych themselves out by having it so easy on the par threes and par fours."

These bets, like the Nassaus, are negotiated on the first tee. The Archivist has no set amount for his betting: "You have to take what comes along. You can't get on the first tee and figure you're going to get $1000 a side in Nassaus. You're just going to scare the hell out of people and you won't have either a bet or a golf game." So if *they* don't start out with big bets, he doesn't. He takes the action as it develops: "Maybe $20 a side in Nassaus, maybe 100 bucks a side." But his low-keyed, low-profile posture is deceptive. He looks for a lot of action beyond the first tee. "Before we're through, I'll be betting 'em on every hole and every shot. I'll bet whether they'll get a birdie, a par, whether they'll sink the putt, who'll be farthest off the tee, first on the green, closest to the cup, everything you can think of." This, too, is part of the psychology of hustling: "A guy who figures 'What the hell, the worst I can do is lose twenty bucks Nassau' winds up standing over a putt and suddenly realizes that I've been 'pyramiding' him and he may have a $1500 putt looking up at him. And that's the putt he's going to blow." In these on-the-course bets, the Archivist again takes advantage of his knowledge of course and hole design as well as what his opponent can do. "If the hole bends right and my pigeon can't hit a controlled fade, I know he's not going to be able to tuck the ball in there close to the hole. Hell, even if the fairway is straight and long but the cup is up there behind the bunkers on the right-hand side of the green. I know he's not going to be able to get up there close to the cup—he's going to be shooting for the left-hand side of the green and start putting across." That means more putts or big trouble: "He hits the first putt so hard it goes off the green and into the bunkers." The Archivist's point is that he can spot so many bets to make that he doesn't have to cheat: He doesn't even have to battle

"A guy who figures 'What the hell, the worst I can do is lose twenty bucks Nassau' winds up standing over a putt and suddenly realizes that I've been 'pyramiding' him and he may have a $1500 putt looking up at him."

"*I know the golf course is a block away!*
Don't rub it in!"

for the big edge on the handicap on the first tee. "I can look like I'm giving something away there and know that I'm going to get it back on the golf course." Or he can make a low-yield Nassau: "It's a prime thing in hustling to make it look like money doesn't mean anything to you. 'OK, if you want to make it easy, let's play ten dollars a side.' Then they don't feel they're being hustled."

He'll do this with all the members of his foursome. He'll do it with other players who may gather at crowded tees late in a round— "if I know them." Thus, what starts out as a foursome might involve six or eight bettors or even more late in a game. "Down there where Trevino plays out of"—Horizon City Country Club in El Paso— "they'll go out in foursomes or sixsomes and wind up with twelvesomes on some of those holes. Hell, when they come off those tees in their golf carts, it looks like a Roman chariot race."

So what starts out as a modest piece of action can build to something pretty wild. "Presses, double presses"—double or nothing, quadruple or nothing—"and parlays, anything you can think of, with half a dozen, maybe a dozen guys in the action; you can be going for a couple of thousand bucks by the end of a round." He remembers he built the action from a "little Nassau" to more than $5000 in one round in Miami. "You can afford to give a little—let a guy think he's taking you for $20 early in the game—when you know what's going to come later on." Of course, he's not the only guy doing the betting. He's encouraging everybody to cross-bet, in order to step up the action and yet not look like the guy who's "making" the game. "The big thing is to have a good memory. That's where I come in handy. I can remember all the bets, not only my own but what the other guys have laid. So I come in pretty handy for them—I can handle the traffic. And when the payoffs are made, it's not all one-way traffic, money coming into my hand and nobody else's. The money's getting passed around. Only I'm not passing it out as much as the other guys."

He maintains the same low profile when he spots a guy cheating. "I guess I've seen all the tricks," he says. Not just the gross: washing a ball with a vigorous rackety-rax—in a wooden ball washer near the tee—when an opponent is in his backswing, jingling coins in a pocket as he stands over a critical putt. "The real sneak is the guy who's pulling something out where he figures he can't be seen." In the fairway, for example, a golfer is allowed to clear away any impediment—a twig, a stray leaf, perhaps a branch or even a food wrapper—from behind the lie of the ball. But not in the sandy rough: He cannot clear pebbles or wet-hardened clumps of sand or anything else from behind the ball. Indeed, you are not even allowed to touch the sand with anything but the soles of your shoes.

"But I've seen guys bend over and look as if they're clearing out a twig or a leaf—like they don't know the rule against it—and they'll stick out a finger or two and brush the sand behind the ball. Dig out a little trench behind the ball with that finger, so that the impact side of the ball sits up free and clear on the sand." Or he'll see other golfers go into a grassy rough and violate another rule—that of not pressing the grass down behind the ball so that, in effect, the rough is cleared from behind it. "But I'll see guys choose a wood for what is clearly an iron shot, go in and address the ball, and then 'change their mind' and call for an iron instead," says the Archivist. "They think I don't know what they're doing: They're taking that wood and leaning down on it while they're 'addressing' the ball, and pressing the grass flat behind it." He rarely calls them on it, unless it's a key shot that'll cost him a lot of money. "Usually, I pick out the feistiest, most uptight guy in the foursome and I point out to him what's going on. And I let *him* go up to the kink and call him out. I don't need enemies—I just let them fight it out among themselves. When it's to my benefit."

So the high-class hustle demands identity but not celebrity. No prominence, no eminence, no salience. The wanderers of the past can make a big point of hustling only if they're willing to settle into a penny-ante life. So says the Archivist. "I'm a professional," he says. "I made a study of the field. I gathered what the scholars said about it and I found something cerebral in it"—i.e., the psychology of the hustle as well as the hustle itself. "I found a new form of the art and a way to make it fill my own life. I can go on doing it all my life—I can be a gentleman golfer for the next 40 years." He finished the last of his scotch and water and the night lights came on. "Nobody is going to give me a Nobel Prize for it," he said. "But I don't have to sit here and drink all night." So he got up and left.

*"You Gordons would do anything to win
a bet, wouldn't you?"*

PLAYBOY'S PARTY JOKES

THE MAN STRANDED on a desert island could not believe his eyes when a beautiful woman in scuba gear appeared on the shore. She smiled and said, "I'll bet you could use a cigarette." Unzipping the sleeve of her wet suit, she pulled out one and handed it to him.

"I'll bet," she continued when the man had finished his smoke, "you haven't had a nice, cold beer in a long time." Unzipping the leg of her wet suit, she pulled out a brew and gave it to the grateful man.

When he had drained the last drop, the shapely woman unzipped the front of her wet suit. "I'll bet," she purred, "it's been a long time since you played around."

"You mean," the man gasped, "you've got *golf clubs* in there?"

• • •

THE GOLFER HAD BEEN playing badly, so he went to a psychiatrist who suggested he relax by playing a round without a ball. "Do everything you normally would, but use an imaginary ball," the shrink said.

The golfer tried it the next day. He stepped onto the first tee and imagined he hit a 260-yard drive. Then, walking the course, he imagined a fine approach shot to the green and a short putt for a birdie.

As he approached the 18th tee, he met another golfer who had seen the same psychiatrist and was also playing without a ball. They decided to play the last hole together and bet $100 on the outcome.

The first golfer swung at his imaginary ball and announced that it had gone 280 yards right down the middle of the fairway. The second golfer matched his drive.

The first fellow then took out his five iron, took a swing and shouted, "Look at that shot! It went right over the pin and backspin brought it right back into the hole, I win!"

"No, you don't," the second golfer said. "You hit my ball."

"That's enough of your putter, baby—use your driver!"